GROW, BUILD, SELL, LIVE

Praise for *Grow, Build, Sell, Live*:

'Crispin has been helping me to develop my agency for the past six years. Thanks to his suggestions I've made major changes in financial, HR and client management. This has transformed our profitability and enabled me to develop a sustainable business that is helping me achieve my personal life goals. I recommend Crispin and Richard's book to anyone intent on building a great agency.'

Patrik Schober, CEO PRAM Consulting, Prague

'Agency leaders like me need a practical book like this. We have so many things to do day by day and hardly have time for our own professional development. But if we want to build a successful, long lasting business, we cannot stop learning and strengthening our knowledge. This book is a perfect resource for that.'

Andras R Nagy, Owner of Probako Communication, Former Chairman of Worldcom EMEA region

'This guide will not only inspire, but more importantly also focus minds on what really matters at an agency, giving owners renewed vigour to actually get out of bed in the morning. It should help distil disparate ideas into a coherent strategic overview, ensuring companies have a clear purpose to be successful.'

Henry Griffiths, Partner, Little Red Rooster PR

'Running an agency has unique challenges, stresses and opportunities for growth. If I'd read this book 15 years ago, I would have made many different decisions, and reached them with more focus and less turmoil. In

*short, reading this book is one of the best investments
you can make in yourself, and your business.*

*Crispin Manners' understanding of agency strategy,
operations are top-of-the-game. His insights into the
nuances that can accelerate or impede agency
performance, and the choices owners may make, are
based on years of direct experience in the centre of
the storm, which is rare and valuable. I've read
several books on agency performance in the 30 years
I've run my firm, and this is possibly the most
incisive, and useful.'*

Amy Bermar, President, Corporate Ink, Boston, USA

*'This book is a great resource for PR agency
owners – and anyone wishing to build a great
agency. I wish I had read it when I founded my
agency. Every business leader working in a people-
based business should have a look at it, the real-life
examples can be helpful in every stage of the agency
life-cycle: start-up, growth, sale or succession.'*

Diego Biasi, Founder & CEO, BPRESS, Italy

*'Whether you're an existing or wannabe PR agency
boss, stop whatever you are doing and buy this book.
It's so good, I wish I'd written it. With explicit
guidelines on how formalising your purpose can
revolutionise your culture and cashflow, and a must-
read section on innovation, it's the best investment
you'll make this year. Hands off my copy!'*

Sarah Waddington, Founder and Editor of
#FuturePRoof and Vice-president of the
Chartered Institute of Public Relations

GROW, BUILD, SELL, LIVE: A PRACTICAL GUIDE TO RUNNING AND BUILDING AN AGENCY AND ENJOYING IT

PRCA Practice Guides

BY

RICHARD HOUGHTON
CRISPIN MANNERS

United Kingdom – North America – Japan – India
Malaysia – China

Emerald Publishing Limited
Howard House, Wagon Lane, Bingley BD16 1WA, UK

First edition 2019

Reprints and permissions service
Contact: permissions@emeraldinsight.com

British Library Cataloguing in Publication Data
A catalogue record for this book is available from the British
Library

ISBN: 978-1-78756-886-0 (Print)
ISBN: 978-1-78756-883-9 (Online)
ISBN: 978-1-78756-885-3 (Epub)

ISOQAR certified
Management System,
awarded to Emerald
for adherence to
Environmental
standard
ISO 14001:2004.

Certificate Number 1985
ISO 14001

INVESTOR IN PEOPLE

CONTENTS

LIST OF FIGURES

FOREWORD

Agency leaders spend the majority of their time on three areas – their people, their clients and on new business. These are all important levers for consultancy growth. But all too often, agency owners forget two more essential tools for growth: attention to the numbers and investment in their leaders. The consultancy leadership role can seem like an endless stream of fires to put out. It can leave leaders feeling as if their team, or their clients, are running their business rather than themselves. That's where this book comes in.

Grow, Build, Sell, Live features practical and implementable advice and tools to address the day-to-day reality of running a successful agency. In addition to giving guidance on people, clients and new business, the book covers leadership and the numbers in detail to ensure leaders have the tools and knowledge to be in control. The content draws on proven approaches, helpful science and real-life examples to give practical recommendations to improve readers' ability to achieve the controlled growth which is essential to agency success.

If you are thinking about starting your own agency, have started one and hit your first round of growing pains, or are a veteran looking for an exit, this book is for you. It will appeal to current and aspiring agency owners who want to understand their choices and take control of their agency.

PRCA Practice Guides are a series of practical and readable books that provide PR and communications professionals, new and experienced alike, with hands-on guidance to help them succeed in a highly competitive sector. Written by experienced practitioners who have already succeeded in the world of PR and communications, *PRCA Practice Guides* offer powerful insights into the challenges of the modern industry and guidance on how to navigate your way through them.

Francis Ingham
Director General, PRCA
Chief Executive, ICCO

ACKNOWLEDGEMENTS

Crispin Manners

I would like to acknowledge some special people who helped in many ways throughout my career: my father, Norman Manners, who taught me everything about the craft of Public Relations and Alan Atherton, Alan Cormack, Sir Herbert Durkin and Sir Frank Rogers who provided wise counsel and much encouragement.

Richard Houghton

I would like to thank Ian Berrido and Barry Leggetter for spending the time to mentor me in the practice of public relations, Theresa Guppy who patiently coached me on the business of PR consultancy and John Gage for so generously sharing his expertise and experience.

INTRODUCTION

BUILDING A GREAT AGENCY – ONE CHOICE AT A TIME

A practical guide for Owners, CEOs and MDs on how to build a successful consultancy so it gives you what you want from your life

Every three minutes, somewhere in the world, a new PR/communications consultancy is born. That's an extra 175,200 potential competitors every year. In every one of those companies there is a leader like you. Someone full of hope, excitement and maybe, a little trepidation. Five years later, about half of those consultancies will have survived – so that's an additional 438,000 competitors.

No wonder running a PR agency can be hard work.

So, if you are thinking about starting your own consultancy, have started one and hit your first round of growing pains, or are a veteran looking at an exit, this book is for you.

In it you'll find practical and implementable advice and tools to address the day-to-day reality of running a successful consultancy – without a lot of the stress and angst that usually goes with it.

1.1. DON'T FORGET YOU MATTER TOO

If you're like most agency leaders, you'll spend most of your time on three areas – your people, your clients and new business. These are all important levers for consultancy growth. But two other areas need at least the same level of attention – the numbers and YOU. Yes you. Too often the owner/leader doesn't invest enough in their own needs – and this lack of 'investment' in themselves can really hurt when the business needs them the most.

So, in addition to giving guidance on people, clients and new business, we've made sure that you and the numbers are both covered off in detail.

1.2. BUILDING A GREAT AGENCY ONE CHOICE AT A TIME

We talk a lot about choices – and the fact that we all have more choice about what happens next than we think we have.

The business model for a consultancy is a simple one. We package expertise, creativity and contacts as 'time' and then sell it. The reality, as we all know, is that delivering on this model, day-in-day-out, is demanding at best and exhausting at worst.

When you grow at 34% compound for a decade, or reshape an ailing agency for a global group (as we have done), you learn a lot of lessons. We've experienced the inevitable lows created by day-to-day issues, such as staff churn, unreasonable clients and price-cutting competitors. But we've also enjoyed the highs that agency life can deliver — doing great work, winning awards and seeing good people develop into great people.

The consultancy owner/CEO/MD role can seem like an endless stream of issues to handle and fires to put out. It can leave you feeling as if your team, or your clients, are running your business — rather than you. And that your company runs your life, rather than helping you to create the life you want to lead.

That's where this book comes in.

1.3. TOOLS AND GUIDANCE TO PUT YOU MORE IN CONTROL OF THE CHOICES YOU MAKE

We've put together practical and implementable guidance on how to manage your consultancy so that you have more control and, most importantly, so that it gives you what you want from your life.

The content draws on proven approaches and some helpful science. It also quotes some real-life examples from leaders we know. We've changed the names to protect the innocent!

We talk a lot about growth. Not because being big is best, but because in our experience, controlled growth is essential to getting the best from your people and your business. How much you grow depends on why you started the business in the first place. Which brings us back to choices.

We wrote this book, not to be prescriptive but to encourage you to think about your choices more, and to think about them earlier.

We want you to understand your choices. We want you to make them conscious rather than unconscious choices. Only then can you control them, rather than have them control you.

Crispin and Richard

CHAPTER 1

THE DANGERS OF TRAVELLING HOPEFULLY AND HOW A PURPOSE BECOMES A PLAN

Issues that may be familiar:

- Wondering why all the hard work doesn't seem to be paying off the way you hoped

- Wondering why it's always you that has to solve the agency's problems

- Wondering why your people don't seem as excited about what the agency does as you are

- Wondering why the clients you want to work for don't seek you out

- Wishing your people would be a bit more proactive

This chapter focuses on both the tangible and intangible outcomes that will make you feel you've achieved something special.

A lot of people start their business with the famous Robert Louis Stephenson quote in mind: 'It's better to travel hopefully than to arrive [updated for brevity's sake]'.

Others start a business because of a 'sliding doors'[1] moment – a choice that created an agency rather than taking another path. Some, in my experience the exceptions, had a clear goal in mind before they opened their doors for business.

So, as you read this chapter, ask yourself. Why did I start (am I starting) my business? What is the Purpose of the business and for me? If you can't recite your Purpose instantly, then we recommend you run a session to define it. And, define the Purpose in terms that mean something important for you (and your family), for clients and your people.

Some of you may say it's obvious, it's to make money. But how much money and by when? And do you care how you make it, or does the type of service you provide matter too? What about the type of clients? Will you work for anyone or are some types of organisations off limits? And what value will you deliver to your clients? Is it tangible value like revenue or intangible value like trust?

Defining both your personal and company Purpose with clarity will provide three valuable outcomes.

- It will give you a framework for guiding your choices and your business plans.

- It will explain the value you deliver to clients and thus make it easier to win them.

---

[1] *Sliding Doors* is a 1998 British-American romantic drama film written and directed by Peter Howitt and starring Gwyneth Paltrow and John Hannah. The film alternates between two parallel universes, based on the two paths the central character's life could take depending on whether she catches a train, and causing different outcomes in her life.

- And, it will help you to attract people who are motivated by delivering the company Purpose.

1.1. A FRAMEWORK FOR MAKING CHOICES

By defining your company Purpose, you will create a decision-making framework that will make your future choices and decisions much easier. This is because of a psychological effect that aids decision-making that Robert Cialdini[2] calls *commitment and consistency*. By writing your company Purpose, you are making a commitment to achieving it. Once you have made a commitment, every choice you make will either be consistent or dissonant with achieving the Purpose.

We like to call it the law of little steps. That's because you won't achieve your Purpose in one giant leap. But having made a commitment to it, each choice you make should move you one step closer to achieving it.

In Chapter 10, – 'Make Sure Your Business Is Good Enough to Sell – From Day One' – we mention Ian and how he transformed his business by establishing a personal Purpose for the business. In his case, this was earning enough to send his two children to university in the USA. About a year after he defined his personal Purpose, Ian asked if I thought he should take a part-time Chairman's role at a membership organisation. I reminded him of his personal Purpose and asked him if he thought the distraction caused by the role would be consistent with achieving his personal Purpose. He said it would not. But then he mentioned a new factor – he wanted to make his parents proud and thought

---

[2]https://en.wikipedia.org/wiki/Robert_Cialdini

such a prestigious role would be consistent with this goal but not with his original personal Purpose.

The fact that he chose to take the position shows that making his parents proud should have been a part of his original personal Purpose because it is a powerful driver for him.

In hindsight, taking the role was indeed a distraction. Ian's business suffered because he lost clients while his attention was elsewhere. We're not sharing that story to show how smart we are. We are including it to encourage you to really think about what matters to you. If Ian had included the pride of his parents in the original personal Purpose i.e. 'my business needs to enable me to put my children through university in the USA and make my parents proud', he would have taken other choices (such as ensuring he had a strong deputy to oversee clients while he was away, or waiting until he had this person in place before taking up this role). This would have helped to ensure that his business didn't suffer while he fulfilled the chairman role.

1.2. USING YOUR PURPOSE TO ATTRACT THE RIGHT TALENT

Research shows that people are more energised, productive and happy if they buy-in to the Purpose of their employer. I've heard agency owners say that they hate the fact some people treat their work like a job and show no real passion. But the same owners usually can't provide an explicit and transparent company Purpose that would inspire people to go the extra mile. Nor do they make it completely explicit how the daily actions of every employee help to deliver that Purpose.

We know some of you are probably thinking: 'Hey, we promote widgets or food — we're not exactly solving world famine. So how can our Purpose inspire people.'

Below you will see two different Purpose statements that could apply to the same agency. Each one is likely to attract different types of people:

Statement A: *Our Purpose is to help food companies grow through award-winning creative communications.*

Statement B: *Our Purpose is to help to reduce the obesity burden on the NHS by helping food companies to inspire consumers to adopt healthier lifestyles.*

> *By making your company Purpose as explicit as possible you will give people reasons to join you **and** to want to come to work every day.*

By making your company Purpose as explicit as possible, you will give people reasons to join you and to want to come to work every day.

Statement A is likely to attract people who are motivated by being creative and by being associated with a famous agency. Statement B is likely to attract people who are motivated by healthy living and making a difference to society.

Neither is better than the other. But you have a choice over which agency you want to run and your company Purpose should describe that explicitly.

1.3. ATTRACTING THE RIGHT CLIENTS

In 'Introduction' we highlighted how many agencies are created and how many subsequently fail. Running an agency is tough because there is always so much competition for clients. So, it makes sense to explain your value in a way that accentuates your difference. Defining your company Purpose will help you to do that. It should also deliver other value too – such as reducing the cost of sales.

Some of you may say that Statement B isn't a great statement because it will deter some food companies from choosing the agency. But if you care about healthy living, and making a difference to society, you wouldn't want to work for brands that contribute to the diabetes pandemic. So, in this case, deterring an unhealthy food brand from choosing you would be a good thing. It will reduce your cost of sale by saving time that would be wasted pursuing a brand which would be completely dissonant with your Purpose. However, those food companies who want to promote healthy living will know that your agency shares their goal and will seek you out.

1.4. A COMBINATION OF PERSONAL AND CORPORATE, TANGIBLE AND INTANGIBLE

As you can see, you will need to establish your personal reasons for creating your agency. This should include describing what your firm will look like when you've achieved your goals. Will it have to be famous or just very profitable? Will it need to be big or just enable you to do great work for great clients?

Having this clear picture is very important as it will help you to make the right choices.

We know another agency owner called Ray. He didn't think about his end goals. He had a lot of fun growing his agency. He enjoyed the accolades that came with it. And for about a decade, he knocked back approaches to buy his agency. He did that because he thought he had more to achieve.

The problem was he hadn't defined what that was. Some of you might say what's the problem with that. After all, he had fun growing his agency. But the problem for Ray was that eventually he got tired. And as he tired, his agency ran out of steam too. Then he thought it might be time to sell. But suddenly there were no suitors because they prefer to buy agencies when they are on the rise (see Chapter 10 on being good enough to sell).

So, it's important to work out what you want from your business — both the tangible and intangible outcomes that will make you feel you've achieved something special.

It's also important to define your Purpose, so people — clients and employees —value it too.

By defining it explicitly, it will enable you to make conscious choices that are consistent with your aims. That way you won't be travelling hopefully.

Even if you don't arrive at exactly the destination you defined at the beginning, you'll understand why you made the choices you did and that will leave you more contented.

1.5. TURNING A PURPOSE INTO A PLAN

Once you've defined your public Purpose, you'll need to translate that into a plan that everyone in the business believes they can implement through the work they do every day.

It's vital to success that your people understand the destination for the business and the steps that need to be taken to get there. As a result, the Purpose statement needs to be backed up by something that gets everyone aligned and engaged.

We promised to provide some practical tools. The Alignment Framework on page 14 is a tool that we've found very useful. It is based on a method called OGSM[3] which we've evolved and simplified.

1.6. PROVIDING A SENSE OF PURPOSE WITH THE ALIGNMENT FRAMEWORK

You should develop an Alignment Framework for the company that describes the journey that your company is on. This will enable each department/team to create their own version by selecting the Outcomes, Strategies, Actions and Metrics (OSAM) that are most important for their department or team.

As you can see, there are five levels to this framework.

Level 1 — A single-defining Destination. You may need to define further phrases like agency of choice, so that, it's clear to everyone what this means.

Level 2 — A few Outcomes (usually 2—4) that will help to get you to your destination. Again, these would be defined in more detail. For example, colleague engagement might be defined as ensuring that everyone in the business works well together in teams, and across teams, in a way that supports physical and mental well-being and delivers increased productivity and innovation. The Outcomes are the signposts that will keep you pointed in the right direction.

Level 3 — A few Strategies that will deliver each Outcome. So, for colleague engagement, you could have a Strategy to 'Drive employee engagement' and another to 'Create a personal development process'. Further

---

[3]https://en.wikipedia.org/wiki/OGSM

definition of these titles will explain what they mean for your agency.

Level 4 – A few 'Actions' that will be taken to achieve each Strategy. Again, these would be explained in more detail. For example, in **Figure 1**, we have identified three actions to drive employee engagement. Selecting an employee engagement platform to automate the process, could be seen as self-explanatory but, we recommend that you explain why you are doing this. For example, you might say: 'We want to ensure that everyone has the opportunity to provide anonymous feedback so that no issues go unnoticed. And, we want to automate the way we capture feedback so we can involve the team in the development of the business.' The Actions are the methods you will use to get to your destination with greater certainty and speed.

Level 5 – A few Metrics that will be used to confirm that each Action is delivering the right value. In **Figure 1**, we have identified four metrics to prove that the employee engagement action is delivering the right value. Each metric would be assigned targets for the quarter or year, depending on how often you refresh the framework. The Metrics are the milestones you will pass on the way that shows you are still on track to reach your destination.

1.7. MAKING THE ALIGNMENT FRAMEWORK WORK FOR EVERY EMPLOYEE

If you look at **Figure 1**, without additional explanation, some employees may feel that they can't influence the achievement of some of the Actions, Strategies or Outcomes.

Figure 1. An Alignment Framework.

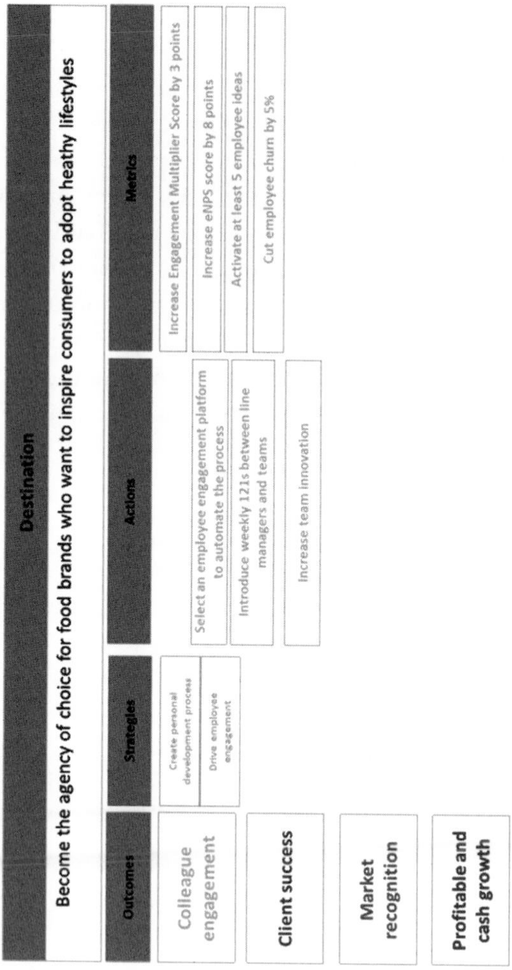

For example, some may feel they can't help to increase team innovation.

Therefore, we recommend that once a company version of the framework has been agreed, team level versions are created with team participation. This will enable each team to identify specific actions they will take to achieve the Outcomes.

In the case of profit and cash growth, account directors and account managers might identify that they can help the company get paid more quickly by building strong relationships with clients that moves your agency up the payment list. They could also go on negotiation skills training, so they can negotiate better supplier terms to reduce the cost of bought-in services and therefore increase the profit contribution from a project.

1.8. WHY IS BUILDING AN ALIGNMENT FRAMEWORK WORTH THE EFFORT?

We're sure the more action and less process-oriented amongst you may be thinking this all sounds a bit unnecessary. But before you discount it, think about choices — not just your choices but those of your people. Choices are the building blocks of success — or failure. It makes sense to help your people make the right choices every day. The Framework will help them to do that so that they become progressively more proactive as they become more confident that they are doing things that bring the company destination closer.

> *If you can increase the productivity of every person by just 10%, the impact could be transformational.*

Think also about the performance of your business. If you can increase the productivity of every person by just 10%, the impact could be transformational. Getting everyone to strive together, because they are aligned around a common Purpose, will see you get to your destination more quickly and with greater certainty.

By involving employees in the creation of team frameworks, you will get much higher levels of commitment to achieving the agreed actions – remember the law of little steps. You will also help to establish priorities by agreeing with each team which actions are the most important. This, in turn, will increase both company and personal effectiveness because it will enable employees to be proactive because they understand what actions matter most and can focus on delivering them.

Providing this level of clarity is vital to satisfying the way our brains work. In Chapter 2 on people, we explain the neuroscience behind why ensuring everyone understands the Purpose is so essential to personal and collective success.

1.9. LINKING THE PURPOSE TO PERSONAL DEVELOPMENT

Research shows that employees prefer organisations who invest in their personal development. Some organisations translate this into spending money on training. While training can be helpful, it's vital that it is training with a purpose.

We recommend that you make a very tight connection between the Alignment Framework and an employee's Personal Development Plan (PDP). To do this, it makes sense to include a copy of the Agency Alignment Framework and the relevant Team Alignment Framework with each employee's PDP. And, it makes sense to focus personal objectives on achieving some of the Outcomes and Actions in the Alignment Framework. In this way, personal development is linked to achieving business outcomes – not development for development's sake.

As you can see, if you make the Purpose run through everything you do, it will make achieving your goals much easier and more enjoyable. In the absence of the clarity that this provides, your employees will not be able to perform at their best and your agency will suffer from that collective inefficiency and ineffectiveness.

1.10. CONNECTING THE PURPOSE TO A TRADITIONAL BUSINESS PLAN

There are lots of books and templates for business plans. The UK government even has a web page dedicated to providing guidance.[4] So, we won't dedicate space in this book for replicating what you can easily find elsewhere.

The key thing to remember is that your Purpose should shape your plan. Without a clear Purpose, you will run the risk that your business plan will shape your life. That's because traditional business plans tend to focus on very tangible things, such as: what growth rate you want, how much space you will need, how many people, which equipment, etc. If you don't have your Purpose very clearly defined, it's easy for you to lose sight of what you are trying to achieve and for the numbers to take over.

For example, if you are building a three-year plan and you decide you want to grow at 10% a year, this will automatically flow through into the need for extra space, people and

---

[4]https://www.gov.uk/write-business-plan

equipment. But what if that extra growth moves you from being a 15-person business to a 20-person business? This may not sound like it's a big change but, we've found that at about 20 people you cross an invisible threshold from being a small business to becoming a big business.

We realise that this makes no sense in terms of the usual size categories for businesses. However, just think for a minute about the way a business of up to 15 people is run. Usually, there are very few written-down systems and processes. Communication is often by osmosis because everyone can hear what is going on and 'just knows' what's expected. It feels like a tight-knit team.

But add a few more people into the mix and suddenly you need a whole array of processes. You'll certainly need internal communications processes to make sure everyone knows what is going on. You'll need much more rigorous financial processes to make sure costs are controlled and clients invoiced correctly. You'll need HR processes to ensure appraisals happen on time — now they are shared around the management team.

All of which is fine if your Purpose has set your destination as becoming a 100-person agency. But what if you're the sort of person that wants to have a process-light business? What if you want to focus on client work rather than admin? Suddenly, you've found yourself leading a business that just doesn't feel like the business you want to run.

Does this mean business plans — and particularly the fact-based parts of them — are a waste of time? Absolutely not. It's essential you scope out the future needs of the business — particularly, in terms of the capital and cash flow requirements this creates. But identifying future needs shouldn't be a theoretical exercise. It should be a function of achieving the Purpose.

> *This means you may need to recruit because you are **not** growing rather than because you are! Recognising this will mean you have a smart recruitment strategy that attracts the right level of skills and experience to replace those who move on.*

For example, if you want to keep the business below the 20-person threshold, the business planning process will need to take account of the fact that you won't be creating as much 'headroom' for bright and ambitious people. So, it's likely that some people will want to leave to progress in their career. This means you may need to recruit because you are **not** growing rather than because you are! Recognising this will mean you have a smart recruitment strategy that attracts the right level of skills and experience to replace those who move on.

And, if you're planning for people to leave, it would make sense to have a strategy that they leave as an advocate for your agency; so that they help you achieve some of your other key Outcomes after they have gone.

1.11. USE YOUR ALIGNMENT FRAMEWORK TO INSTRUCT YOUR BUSINESS PLAN

The Alignment Framework will also instruct your business plan. Take the Outcome of Market Recognition. This could include two Strategies – *win awards* and *increase visual capability*. Both have implications for the business plan.

Increasing visual capability could mean hiring new skills. Or it could mean reskilling the existing team. Or both. Or it could mean outsourcing the visual elements. But if you did that, what would that mean to how the team feel about more visual work. Would they engage with it or just think their job hasn't changed?

Winning awards means time dedicated to something else will need to be switched to the award entry process. Or you could outsource the process. Either way there is not just a cost implication but also a team engagement implication. If winning awards isn't part of the team's job, then they may not design their campaigns to be award-winning from the outset.

> *In our experience, every minute spent on developing a clear Purpose and Alignment Framework will save years of wasted effort across the entire team.*

In our experience, every minute spent on developing a clear Purpose and Alignment Framework will save years of wasted effort across the entire team.

If the choices you make are just cost or efficiency driven, they are unlikely to deliver against the Outcomes. The Framework will remind you that these actions have strategic importance and therefore need to become part of daily activity.

CHAPTER 2

IF YOU'RE RUNNING A PEOPLE BUSINESS, THEN MAKE PEOPLE YOUR BUSINESS

Issues that may be familiar:

- It's hard to attract talent into your agency
- Your staff churn is higher than you would like
- You don't have the right mix of people to grow your agency
- Some of the people you have seem to drain your energy
- Some seem to leave the moment you promote them

We've both encountered agencies which treat people like commodities. It's not a model that motivates us. So, this chapter is dedicated to an approach that reflects the chapter's heading.

So, how do you run an effective people business by making people your business? We've been asked a lot of questions about people. Some we couldn't print. We've identified the

five that come up most often below and added some thoughts
on how you might want to answer them.

As you might imagine, many of our answers link to our
chapters on culture and purpose. There are no perfect
answers because every business is different. The best
approach is to answer the questions in the context of the purpose you have set for your business and for yourself. We provide some thoughts which may help you to make the right
choices for you and your business.

2.1. HOW DO I ATTRACT THE RIGHT PEOPLE?

The answer to this question depends on the definition of
'right'. If 'right' means people who do a great job, then our
advice is to hire people for roles where they can shine. This
means making sure you match natural behavioural preferences to the demands of a role. As an example, if you need
someone to carry out in-depth research, an extrovert with a
short attention span may struggle to do a great job. They
might be able to do so in short bursts but would soon lose
interest.

There are two ways you can reduce your chances of getting it wrong.

- **The first is to create a behavioural profile for the role.**
  Then you can use a psychometric[1] test to check if
  candidates have the natural behavioural preferences to
  meet the needs of the role. It won't guarantee a perfect
  person, but it will help you to avoid a complete
  mismatch.

---

[1]If you want a low-cost psychometric test to help with recruitment, then
use this link https://onva.co.uk/c-me/

- **The second is to avoid the perils of unconscious bias.**
  It's important to recognise that we all tend to like
  communicating with people who communicate like we do.
  This means that we all have an unconscious bias towards
  people who behave like us. As a result, you run the risk of
  not selecting people who are perfect for a role simply
  because they are not 'your type of person'.

Once you recognise your propensity for unconscious bias,
you can try and adapt how you act when recruiting, or you
can involve colleagues who may be closer to the desired style
of behaviour. You can also use the behavioural profile for the
role to help you make a more informed, conscious decision
about who is best.

The other way to attract the right people is, as we covered
in the Purpose chapter, to make your Purpose as explicit as
possible. This will attract people who are inspired by the
Purpose and therefore much more likely to perform well if
they join you. Not only will an explicit Purpose make recruitment more effective, but it will also give people reasons to
want to come to work every day.

2.1.1. Successful Recruitment Is a Trust Purchase

You can make attracting the right people even easier by creating a workplace culture that turns employees into advocates
for the business. These advocates or 'fans' will actively recommend working at your firm. Remember, when someone
joins your company, they are making a trust purchase. The
more you can build trust in your brand through the recommendations of people new recruits will work with, the easier
it will be to win the battle for talent.

2.2. HOW LONG SHOULD I EXPECT
PEOPLE TO STAY?

The long answer is that you should expect people to stay for as long as you give them reasons to come back every day. The 'reasons' connect very closely with the SCARF model we cover in more detail in the Culture chapter.

- **Status** – If an employee feels like they or their team does work that is valued by you and the business, they will have a positive sense of status. For example, if your company has a B2B tech team and a consumer lifestyle team, but you only ever talk about the lifestyle team's work, then the tech team will feel less valued.

  I've known agency leaders say things like: 'Surely they know we value them? After all their team represents a third of the business.' The trouble is that expecting people to read between the lines just doesn't work. You need to be very explicit if you want people to know that you value their contribution.

- **Certainty** – If something changes in your business but the implications of this change are not explained, this will cause anxiety. In the absence of explicit explanations, people often create their own version of the truth. They will then make choices based on what they believe to be the truth of the matter.

  For example, if a new person joins but the reasons aren't clearly explained, some people may feel that the career path they thought existed has just been closed off. Just as with the Status example above, explicit messages are essential to provide employees with the 'certainty' they crave.

  This also applies to their day job. Providing very clear briefs is essential to satisfy the need for certainty. A clear brief removes the potential for anxiety that the wrong thing will be delivered.

- **Autonomy** – If an employee feels like there are very clear parameters within which they are expected to operate, they will be able to satisfy their need for feeling in control and therefore feel able to take decisions. Providing these parameters also supports the certainty need.

  Does this mean that you need to create very tight systems and processes for everything that happens in your business? No. But it does mean that you need to understand the need for autonomy, especially if you want people to be proactive.

  As my business grew, we recognised the need to establish clear parameters for people. One of my co-directors thought this would inhibit people because his natural preference is to have no boundaries. But what he finds constraining would be liberating for someone with an opposite set of preferences.

  So, what's the moral of this story? It's simply that establishing parameters is essential and that the parameters must be the right ones for different behavioural preferences. In the case of my co-director, this involved a very simple description of his area of responsibility – as expressed by his team's Alignment Framework. For those that need the reassurance of clearly expressed 'if this then that' parameters (the comfort of the familiar if you like), it will mean a more detailed explanation is required.

2.2.1. Don't Get Caught Out by the Churn Points or Make a Promotion a Reason to Leave

The shorter answer to the question is that, if you recruit graduates, we have identified three 'churn' points once someone has completed their trial period. These 'churn' points come at two, four and 10 years. As your employees approach these 'anniversaries', it makes sense to check how they are feeling so you can refresh their desire to stay if it's needed.

The churn points are also indicative of why it's essential to ensure you have a personal development process that includes frequent contact. We cover this in more detail below.

In the absence of regular check-ins with their line manager, we've found employees will think they have few choices about the way their career can develop. In many cases, employees have a very binary view of development — it's up or out. Some believe that going up the proverbial career ladder is the only way to progress, when going sideways might be much better for them and the business.

> *In the absence of regular check-ins with their line manager, we've found employees will think they have few choices about the way their career can develop.*

Frequent contact, rather than relying on six monthly or annual appraisal meetings, enables you to be more in tune with how an employee is feeling and to explain the implications of the next job up the ladder.

For example, the move from account manager to account director brings with it some significant changes. Usually it brings revenue responsibility, which in turn means taking the lead on sales activity. Some people who are great account managers may not have the natural preferences to be effective in this new 'sales' role. This means they may not enjoy their new responsibilities. So, a promotion may actually set them up to fail. In our experience, employees underestimate what a more senior role entails until they have been exposed to it. So, explaining these implications to employees is essential.

Because these churn points exist, it also makes sense to have a recruitment plan which is tuned to attracting talent during periods when it's possible you may lose some people.

2.3. HOW DO I RECRUIT FOR GROWTH?

This is a very interesting question because the answer requires a holistic approach to building a team.

Both Richard and I learnt early in our careers that it's very hard to find good people quickly. It's also very hard to find senior people from elsewhere who will be a good fit for your culture. So, the best way to recruit for growth is to recruit with the expectation that people will develop into future leaders.

Growth requires people who can sell. This is not as simple as hiring the proverbial 'rainmaker', but you will need people who are good at the very particular type of selling that is needed in the agency world. Growth also needs people who can earn the trust of their clients and motivate their teams to perform.

That's why I recommend that you create a map of the current team's psychometric profiles.[2] This will highlight any gaps and potential weaknesses in your team when it comes to growing sustainably.

Figure 1 shows an example agency. It highlights some issues for the firm from a growth perspective.

---

[2]The example used is from C-ME™ Profiling Tests which are available at https://onva.co.uk/c-me/

Figure 1. An Agency's Colour Profile.

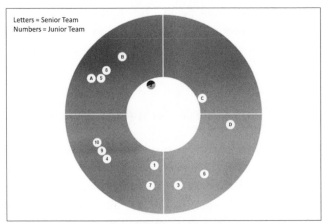

Most of the more junior people represented by numbers in the chart have helper/supporter profiles (the bottom left area of the chart). This is great for roles where steady and reliable performance matters. But these people do not have the natural behavioural preferences to fulfil the role of an account director, without adapting their natural style significantly.

The rest of the more junior team are in the top left quadrant. This means they are very reflective and task oriented. That's great for research and the logistics of project management – but they are unlikely to have the extrovert communication style needed to 'wow' a prospect in a pitch.

This means that, currently, there are no junior people who are likely to grow into a revenue winning and account leadership role.

The senior team also has challenges. Two are on the reflective side in the top left quadrant. That means, they will be able to communicate easily with the junior team in the same quadrant, but they will struggle to do so with those who are in the bottom left of the wheel. Clients will value them for their accuracy and rigour but, without a significant adaptation in their natural behaviour, they lack the relationship and extrovert preferences to be very effective in the classic beauty parade pitching process.

The leader in the top right quadrant will have the drive and focus to win business, but her natural communication style will be the opposite of the people in the bottom left quadrant. This will mean that, unless she adapts her style, she may come across as aggressive and may not motivate the team to deliver effectively for her. Equally, they may seem too passive to her and frustrate her need for momentum.

The net result is that the main burden of new business winning will fall on two people in the top right and right centre zones. They may be capable of winning the business, but without available account directors in the team, the firm may struggle to keep it.

So, to sustain growth, an agency needs:

- People with the right skills and preferences coming through the ranks

- A healthy number of people with top right and right centre profiles, as it is, this profile that has the right mix of relationship, extroversion, ideas and task preferences to be a classic account director/owner

- Leaders and line managers with the communication skills to get the best from the team.

It's also worth saying that you can take the pressure off your recruitment if you have a very effective personal development process and, a brain-friendly culture that motivates people to stay and to perform.

2.4. HOW MUCH SHOULD I SPEND ON TRAINING AND DEVELOPMENT?

If this question is asked because you use a cost-plus approach to budgets, then the answer is probably 'very little'. This is because a piecemeal approach to development is unlikely to work. Consequently, we think you should ask a different question: *How much should we invest in making people more effective?*

If you focus on helping people to become more effective, then you will deliver a very healthy return on investment. Development isn't a 'nice to have'. It's a must have. A survey we ran for a client recently identified that about 60% of employees think it is an employer's responsibility to help them to both upskill and reskill. The same survey uncovered what employees look for in a personal development process. The research showed that employees ask for things like a clear understanding of what is expected from their role, transparency on how they are assessed so they feel it is fair, clarity on what they are allowed to decide for themselves and, recognition of what they have done well. These all correspond to the needs in the SCARF framework, such as certainty, autonomy and fairness. They also want regular coaching.

You can buy time management or effectiveness training courses. They have some value, but it would be best to do so as part of a holistic approach to development. The main elements of this complete approach are as follows:

- A very explicit Purpose brought to life by team Alignment Frameworks and simple, clear definitions of everything in the Framework — see the chapter on Purpose

- A Personal Development Plan for every employee

- Line managers who operate as coaches and have regular check-ins with the people who report to them

- Line managers who adapt their communications style to the needs of each employee.

We have developed a very effective PDP form which ensures that personal development is tightly linked to the Purpose of the business. The approach we recommend is that all personal objectives should be focused at delivering against the Actions in the Alignment Framework. We also recommend that:

- You ask each employee to define who their customer is. The answer here is not as obvious as you might think. Employees might need to satisfy a range of different customer types. It's important that each one recognises who their customer(s) is/are so that meeting customer needs becomes central to everyone's daily activity. Customer could include the following:
  - **Clients**

  - **Partners/suppliers**

  - **The media and other influencers**

  - **Colleagues.** It's very important to include this internal customer and some of the other customer types. Otherwise, employees who have little or no client contact will feel disconnected from the Purpose and have a lesser sense of Status. This will negatively impact their performance.

- You ask employees to write their objectives under three subheadings: Deliver, Delight and Develop.
  - **Deliver:**
    This is the Quantitative element, that is, what will an employee do for their client (internal or external) to

deliver that objective that also delivers against the
Alignment Framework.

○ **Delight:**

This is the Qualitative element and focuses on what
an employee is going to do to delight clients by
delivering that objective.

○ **Develop:**

This is the Personal element and focuses on what the
employee needs to know or learn to be able to deliver the
objective. This is very important because it links personal
development to the needs of the business.

- To ensure fairness is built-in, you ask them to identify any
barriers to achieving this objective. It's important to add
any context to the objective that shows how difficult it
might be. For example, an account director might have a
personal objective of winning £100k of new business, but
his or her team may be short an account manager. So,
unless another account manager is recruited – or an
interim solution found – it may be hard to win all the new
business because there aren't enough people to service it.

If this context isn't added, then the employee may not
feel the assessment at the end of the appraisal period is
fair. Feeling unfairly treated (one of the key elements of
SCARF) can significantly impair performance. It can also
cause people to spread negative messages and to leave. The
survey mentioned above identified that 31% of employees
have left a company because of unfair treatment from a
line manager!

Following this approach will have benefits for the business
and for the employee. For the business, it will mean every
employee is focusing their action on achieving things that will
move the business forward. For the employee, it will satisfy

all five elements of the SCARF framework – see the chapter on Culture. This means that they will be in a much more positive frame of mind – and thus more capable of achieving their objectives.

2.5. THIS PERSON JUST ISN'T PERFORMING ANYMORE, SHOULD I LET THEM GO?

This question is quite often asked about people who were rising stars, but who seemed to have stalled. Martin, an agency owner we know asked this question about April, one of the company's directors, who had just lost three significant clients. April was on a big salary, so was no longer 'paying her way'. She also appeared resistant to focusing on new business, preferring to focus on her remaining clients. Martin is an American, so not subject to the more stringent employment laws operating in the UK and Europe. So, he thought he should 'let April go'. But, only six months earlier, April had the highest client loading of all account owners and was short at least one account manager.

Further questions identified that Martin, until very recently, had been a very hands-on owner who had made all the decisions but was now looking for April and the other directors to 'step up and share the leadership load'. A quick look at their psychometric profiles showed that April and Martin had very similar behavioural profiles. While this can help when people are aligned, it can cause issues when they are not. This is exacerbated in this case by the fact that both Martin and April prefer to be the 'one who decides'.

The problem for Martin is that his natural inclination was to step back in and solve the immediate problem – April. But the real, and much deeper, issue was that he hadn't created real succession in his business by coaching the next generation of leaders how to lead. Nor had he given them the autonomy to address issues before they become terminal problems – such as a client deciding to leave.

So, if you ever want to ask that question, first ask yourself why the person has stopped performing. You may find that it is a symptom of a wider problem that needs solving. Check if you have created alignment in your senior team. And, check that you have learnt how to adapt your communication style to have very effective, rather than combative, interactions. Perhaps most importantly of all, ensure you allocate adequate time to coach your best talent. The best leaders are always the best coaches and best communicators.

Unless you begin to share the load, with people who are happy to carry it, you will create your own glass ceiling. If you want every decision to go through you, that's fine. This book isn't about being right or wrong. It's about making the rights choices to achieve the Purpose you defined for the business and creating an environment in which you can have some fun along the way.

CHAPTER 3

CULTURE MATTERS — IT WILL DETERMINE HOW FAST YOU SUCCEED

Issues that may be familiar:

- You have lots of talented individuals but they don't work as a team
- Your employees don't all understand the direction the agency is heading in
- You can't describe the culture of your agency in ways that everyone understands and buys into
- You seem to be constantly explaining what sort of behaviour you want from your people
- The money you spend on training doesn't seem to deliver the expected improvement in performance

Creating a business that is 'good enough to sell' is not a one-person job. It needs a team of people to make it happen. That sounds obvious. But what does it take to create a team and not just a group of talented individuals? And what does it take for the team to succeed?

Henry Ford summarised neatly what is involved, with this quote: 'Coming together is a beginning. Keeping together is progress. Working together is success.'[1] He went on to say: 'If everyone is moving forward together, then success takes care of itself.'

In 'Introduction', we talked about how every year more competitors arrive to make life more difficult for you. To succeed in this challenging environment, you need to compete effectively. But what does compete really mean? For most people, to compete means to battle with competitors, but the definition of the Latin for compete − *competere* − is different. It means to strive together. We believe this brings the true meaning of being competitive into focus. **If you want to be competitive, you need the whole team to strive together to achieve a common purpose.**

So how do you get everyone moving forward together? You create a purpose that will deliver what you want, both personally and professionally, and describe it in a way that helps you to attract the talent you need to achieve that purpose.

> *Culture is the connective tissue that keeps all the moving parts of your business moving as one and in the right direction.*

But you need to support the purpose with a culture of shared assumptions, values and beliefs, which controls how people behave.

This could sound a bit like a copywriting challenge. Put a team together to identify and capture these beliefs

---

[1] http://www.tbae.co.za/blog/team-building-quotes-from-henry-ford/

and values and the rest will take care of itself. But words alone won't deliver success.

It is the behaviour that the words describe that matters. In many ways, culture is the connective tissue that keeps all the moving parts of your business moving as one and in the right direction.

3.1. THE INGREDIENTS OF AN EFFECTIVE CULTURE

We've identified some of the things below that you should consider if you want to make sure your culture delivers the success you want.

1. **Your culture starts with you.** Your behaviour (and that of the leadership team) defines the culture for your company, so be honest with yourself and start by capturing your own beliefs and values. By doing that, your team will see that what you do is true to the values of the business. If you promise something different to how you behave, you will simply attract people and then disappoint them. Not only is this a waste of time and money but also it will upset you and the people you have misled.

   One CEO we know, let's call him George, wants people to be proactive and take responsibility for things. But George needs to be the one who decides everything. It's impossible for people to be truly proactive if you don't allow them to take any decisions. Are we saying George is wrong to want to be the decision maker? No. But it would be better all round if he made it clear that the culture of his firm would suit people who preferred to work within clearly defined parameters that enabled them to make recommendations but not take decisions. You can't promise one thing and deliver another and expect people to be happy and productive.

2. **The outcomes you value should drive your team's behaviour.** We've seen a lot of teams being busy. That's lots of spinning wheels but no forward motion. Do you explain to the team the top three outcomes you want to achieve in any given period? If you do, then it is much easier for your team to move forward together. It gives them a framework to use to decide what they will do each day. It helps them to know that their actions will achieve the outcomes you value most.

   In our experience, it's a good idea to describe the desired outcomes for the year ahead and then prioritise them every three months. This shorter time window enables people to connect their daily actions with the top priorities. That's why we recommend you develop an Alignment Framework – see Chapter 1 on Purpose.

3. **Does your behaviour make you a friend or a foe?** That may seem an odd question. But, as the old adage goes, the mind works in mysterious ways. In fact, the mind is not mysterious at all. It is hardwired to minimise threat and maximise reward. Our brain automatically (and very quickly) works out if someone is displaying a 'friend' or a 'foe' behaviour. This is a deeply ingrained survival mechanism, and it conditions how people behave at work.

   So, little things you do can derail your best intentions. The things you say and, more importantly, the way you say them, can be received as a 'threat' by your team. This automatically puts people on the defensive. It negatively impacts their ability to make decisions and stops people from being happy and productive.

The reverse is also true. The things you do or say can create a 'reward' reaction. This will automatically mean the team will be open to engaging with you. One science paper describes this as follows: '*Engagement is a state of being willing to do difficult things, to take risks, to think deeply about issues and develop new solutions.*' This is a mindset that can move a business forward. It's a mindset that is essential in an agency if you want to meet client needs and expectations.

3.2. USE SCARF TO ENSURE YOU CREATE A PRODUCTIVE AND HAPPY ENVIRONMENT

We've identified a very neat model to help create a 'reward' culture. If you let it guide how you and your senior team behave, and guide what you say, it will reduce the risk of creating foe or threat reactions in your people. It's called SCARF and was created by David Rock, who coined the term 'Neuroleadership' and is the Director of the NeuroLeadership Institute, a global initiative bringing neuroscientists and leadership experts together to build a new science for leadership development.

We refer to SCARF in our chapter on People. You can find out more by reading this paper.[2]

SCARF is based on five social needs that our brains have: *Status, Certainty, Autonomy, Relatedness and Fairness.* The employee engagement work we have undertaken shows consistently that employees want their leaders to make the company's Purpose much clearer. We like SCARF because it helps business leaders to understand why that matters, and

---

[2]This paper explains Rock's findings (https://neuroleadership.com/portfolio-items/scarf-a-brain-based-model-for-collaborating-with-and-influencing-others/).

therefore, why they need to put real effort behind making it clear. More importantly, SCARF shows why it is essential to explain to each and every employee how their everyday work contributes to achieving that Purpose.

SCARF is a simple framework you can follow. It will help you to give your team the Status, Certainty, Autonomy, Relatedness and Fairness they crave. By doing so, you will increase significantly your chances of success.

Status refers to our social need to understand where we fit in the company. This is because how we are viewed by our colleagues really matters. Feeling like you, or your department, are not essential to the success of the company can negatively impact performance. However, feeling like you make a difference to the company and its customers can trigger a greater sense of capability and energy.

A clear sense of Purpose that explains where people 'fit' – their Status – is therefore vital to personal performance. Finding ways to reinforce this daily, through your behaviour and that of your senior team, is equally vital. As we say in Chapter 2, on people, appearing to favour one team over another through the things you say can be very damaging to the morale and performance of other teams.

Earlier in this chapter we referred to culture as the connective tissue that keeps all the moving parts of your business moving as one and in the right direction. We've seen a lot of agencies put effort into describing their Purpose (Mission, Vision and Values) but then fail to connect the Purpose with all their people-related processes, such as personal development and performance appraisals. So, as you can see in Chapter 1 about Purpose, we recommend that you connect your Personal Development Plans (PDPs) to the company Purpose by including your Alignment Framework in the PDP. By doing so, you will help to reinforce the Status of each employee.

Certainty refers to the human brain's need to know what will happen next. We all want to know what actions will deliver a safe outcome and what actions won't. If things aren't clear and predictable, it creates anxiety, drains energy and makes it harder to solve problems and take decisions. Understanding the company's Purpose is therefore essential to giving employees Certainty about where the company is going and how they contribute to getting there.

But, we're not talking about a diet of strategic stuff. We're talking about a series of small actions that collectively bring certainty on a daily basis. For example, meetings that do not have clear outcomes, and a clear explanation of what will happen next, create uncertainty. An email with an instruction that doesn't explain why a task is important (how it will deliver against the company Purpose) creates uncertainty. PDPs that don't connect personal objectives to the company Purpose create uncertainty. Not having a PDP at all not only falls afoul of the need for Certainty but Status, Autonomy, Relatedness and Fairness too.

If line managers explain what is required, and why it will deliver the required result, this gives people the 'certainty' they are looking for. It gives them the feeling: 'I know exactly how to handle this situation.' Once you focus on creating certainty, you start to realise how your communications behaviour can make a big difference.

We realise that some readers are probably thinking: 'I employ really smart people – they don't need everything to be that explicit.' But, as the neuroscientists have proven, our brains actually do need all five elements of SCARF to be made explicit. Only by doing this will you create a 'reward' culture that enables everyone to perform at their best.

As an example, let's take a hypothetical situation that is no doubt familiar to many of you. Let's imagine a senior team member resigns to go in-house and this threatens one of the agency's largest accounts. Let's imagine that the agency owner instantly goes into recovery mode and begins to take decisions about what to do to buy time with the client while a replacement is recruited.

Nothing wrong with that I hear you cry. But what if the account is big enough to have not one but two account directors. And the second account director – Diane – has very clear views about what would be an effective interim solution and what would make the situation worse. By taking decisions without consulting the second account director – thus presenting her with a fait accompli –the owner would undermine her Status, her Certainty and her levels of Autonomy. This would mean Diane would have no buy-in to the solution and no real commitment to making it work. By exposing her to a situation that would most likely fail, and making it look like she isn't an important part of the solution, the owner would probably encourage her to leave too.

But, what if the owner did consult Diane and adapted the solution based on her feedback. This doesn't mean that the client won't leave. But it does mean that the second account director – energised by a reward reaction in her brain – will try that much harder to keep the account. It also means she is likely to stay – with her status reinforced and with a greater sense of certainty about her own future in the agency.

So, what's the moral of this story? There are two parts to the answer. Firstly, you can't control what you can't control (the behaviour of the client), so focus on trying to control what you can – the behaviour of your people. Secondly, increase the certainty of success by ensuring you trigger a reward reaction in your people by reinforcing the five components of SCARF.

Autonomy refers to our brain's desire to feel that we have choices about what to do and not to do. We all like to feel that we have some level of control over our environment and circumstances. Neuroscience studies have shown that feeling like we can make some autonomous decisions **can increase motivation and engagement by up to five times.** So, it's definitely worth helping the team feel they have clear levels of autonomy.

This isn't about letting employees have complete freedom of choice over what they do every day. But, it is all about giving people a decision-making framework that makes them feel that they are allowed to take their own decisions – to be proactive if you like.

This framework – which we call the Alignment Framework (covered in more detail in Chapter 1 on Purpose) – ensures that people know which are the priority outcomes that the company is trying to achieve to deliver its Purpose. This enables them to ask themselves a very simple question when assessing what work to do: 'Will carrying out this task help us to achieve this or that outcome?' If the answer is yes, then they can be certain it's worth doing. If it's no, then you've effectively given them permission to decide not to do it.

To help people be capable of answering this question, we recommend that each team creates their own version of the Alignment Framework. This will make it explicit which Outcomes, Actions and Metrics matter most to their team – and still help the company reach its destination.

By giving people a sense of autonomy, to deliver a Purpose that means something to them, you will be reinforcing the 'reward' culture that is good for the company and also good for the mental and physical well-being of the individual.

Relatedness refers to our need to feel safe with other people and to feel that we are with friends. Again, for some readers, this may all seem a bit soft and fluffy. Do we really need to like everyone we work with? A study by UCLA[3] suggests

---

[3]Tabibnia and Lieberman (2007).

we do. It shows that social rejection triggers the same reaction in the brain as physical pain.

So, an ill-chosen remark by a line manager or, simply not having regular communication with a line manager, can make people feel like they are on the 'outer'. The failure by a line manager to carry out a personal appraisal, in a way that shows they have not thought about the employee, is a good example of failing to meet the need for Relatedness.

The research, that we refer to in Chapter 2 on people, shows that many line managers operate in a way that makes people feel like they don't belong. It shows that about half of line managers carry out appraisals in a way that would make people feel that they aren't important to the business, such as making it feel like a tick box exercise or carrying out little preparation or follow-up – thus failing to meet the need for Relatedness and Fairness.

So, it's not surprising that the research highlights that 31% of employees have left because of the behaviour of a line manager. We've all heard the adage people don't leave a company, they leave a manager and this research proves it!

Again, you can choose what behaviour you include in your culture. The personal development and performance review process is one of those 'connective tissues' we mentioned above. And, the way that you and your leadership interact with it will decide if your people feel 'related' to your culture or not.

Fairness refers to our need to be treated fairly. According to Rock, being treated unfairly (like Relatedness) activates networks in the brain that register physical pain or pleasure. So, being treated unfairly really does hurt. It is the one reason why people often go to great lengths to right wrongs.

So, if you want a culture where people feel fairly treated, it is essential for managers to avoid doing things that could be interpreted as unfair.

For example, if a line manager carries out a review for one person but postpones a review for another, it could be seen as unfair. You might think that postponing the meeting is just the way of business. That's fine. But when you do so, you also need to recognise the impact the postponement will have. If a postponement is necessary, the line manager will need to explain why it is necessary and automatically schedule the replacement meeting.

> *Unconscious bias can introduce unfairness without you realising it is happening.*

3.3 AVOID UNCONSCIOUS BIAS – IT CAN INTRODUCE UNFAIRNESS WITHOUT YOU REALISING IT IS HAPPENING

Unless leaders have learnt to understand the impact their behaviour has on others, and adapt it accordingly, they run the risk of operating according to the unconscious bias of their natural preferences.

For example, some personality profiles prefer to do everything at a fast pace and tend to think about things at the last minute. As a result, they run the risk of doing two things that are seen as unfair by employees. Firstly, they ask for work to be carried out at the last minute. And secondly, they often give short deadlines for it to be completed – even if there is actually more time available to deliver the task.

Once when we were delivering training on adapting behaviour to the needs of others, the CEO (Julia) had a light-bulb moment. She admitted in the session that she had been doing exactly what we described above – and had thought it a good thing to do!

Julia admitted that she felt that she performed at her best if she put herself under pressure by having very tight deadlines. It was only when she realised that this approach created a 'threat' reaction in her team that she realised that she needed to change. She suddenly appreciated that quite a few members of her team preferred to have more time to think things through, so they could be certain they would deliver a quality output.

Julia realised that her behaviour was hurting her business. It meant that people were stressed when they didn't need to be – making them less productive. It meant that some work wasn't as high quality as it could be and, some work wasn't completed at all. As a result, she had some negative views about some of her team because they missed phoney or ill-considered deadlines.

In short, there were many negative consequences driven by a single behavioural preference. So, Julia decided to make a simple adaptation – to brief earlier. The impact on productivity and morale of this one change was immediate and profound.

3.4. CREATE A COACHING CULTURE

If you want to create an effective culture, we recommend you recognise the difference between training and coaching. We believe you train for skills and you coach for performance. We see a lot of agency leaders dedicate time and budget to training but then feel frustrated that it doesn't deliver a significant improvement in performance.

Training needs to be complemented by coaching where a line manager will give an employee 15 minutes advice and guidance in the context of an immediate work need. It is the frequency of this targeted one-to-one coaching that ticks all five of the SCARF needs. The research we mentioned in Chapter 2 shows how important frequency of coaching contact is to get the best from your people. The top two expectations for how employees want personal development to be run are as follows: to have regular check-ins with their line manager so they know exactly how they are performing and, regular and timely feedback on where they need to improve so they can make the necessary changes before their next appraisal.

The famous saying: *Give a man a fish, and you feed him for a day. Teach a man to fish, and you feed him for a lifetime* is a perfect example of Autonomy in action. It shows why effective managers allocate time to act as a coach, that is taking the time to explain how things are done and why they are done.

So, you have complete freedom of choice about what behaviour you include in your culture. But we recommend you create a coaching culture if you want to create a business where people perform at their best. It will be good for their physical and mental well-being and also great for the business too.

3.5. THERE IS NO SUCH THING AS THE STATUS QUO, SO MAKE SURE YOU MEASURE HOW ENGAGED YOUR PEOPLE ARE ON A REGULAR BASIS

Cultures develop organically over time. Businesses never stand still because the people within them are always changing. These changes come with new people. They also come as people develop and as their life goals alter. This is important when you think about your culture. To succeed, your culture must embrace change if you want to move forward together.

That's why we recommend that you listen to your employees systematically and on a regular basis. We use a tool called

Engagement Multiplier because it creates an engagement score for your company. It does this across the six dimensions that matter most to business success – including purpose, customers and your people. We like it because it helps you understand engagement levels as your business changes and as the people within it change too. It also encourages you to act on the feedback by identifying some actions you will take in the next 90 days. This link between what your people say and what you do next is brilliant at building trust in your leadership. It's also great at helping to build a strong culture where people feel they move as one. You can access a free trial of Engagement Multiplier by following this link[4] https://www.engagementmultiplier.com/en-gb/partner/onva/

So, what's the moral of this chapter? You're more important than you think! Your culture will reflect your beliefs and behaviours. And the success of your culture will depend on whether your behaviour triggers a 'reward' or 'threat' reaction in your team.

---

[4]A free trial of Engagement Multiplier is available here: https://www.engagementmultiplier.com/en-gb/partner/onva/

CHAPTER 4

SUCCESSFUL AGENCIES NEED GOOD LEADERS

Issues that may be familiar:

- Your team doesn't deliver on your plans as you expect

- Your staff turnover is higher than you would like

- The agency is not all pulling in the same direction

- You tell people to do things, but they don't get done

- Things don't seem to happen – even small things – if you aren't involved

Some people find leadership comes naturally. Others need to work at being effective leaders – this chapter is for you.

At the very heart of a successful agency is a motivated team of people. Without the people you don't have a business, you're just left with an expensive office and rapidly depreciating computers and not much else. Motivating and keeping your team facing the same direction, are two of the most important skills that any agency head can have.

The good news is that while the mantle of leadership may not sit comfortably with you, it can be learned, refined and mastered with a little thought, practice and a whole lot of empathy. More of which later.

4.1. FREEDOM IN A FRAMEWORK

If we had to sum up the central role of a leader, it would be to create a framework within which your team members are given the freedom to be their very best, their most proactive, creative and commercial. It is when all the teams feel ownership of what they are doing, and have the resources to deliver, that morale grows, culture solidifies and profits rise.

How wide and detailed the framework you create will depend on the seniority of your team, the current culture and morale, and personalities. We cover this in more detail in our chapters on Purpose and Culture.

4.2. LEADERSHIP VS MANAGEMENT

Before we detail what the component parts of a good leadership framework is, it is worth considering the difference between management and leadership.

As we develop our careers, we move from doing our own work under the direction of a manager, to handling our work plus the management of others. This change is easy for some and tough for others. Those who find delegation hard, or don't enjoy having to give feedback to team members, often struggle to shift up to the manager role. The same is often the case with the move from management to leadership.

We've come across many new MDs and Directors that are trying to lead a division or an agency, exclusively using management techniques rather than a combination of management and leadership.

There are a number of reasons why management is different from leadership, and these include the following:

- Management relies on logic, while Leadership also requires the harnessing of emotion

- Management focuses on today and tomorrow but Leadership also requires a focus on the medium and long-term

- Management demands mastery of detail, while Leadership requires the ability to understand and paint the big picture

- Management requires control of a team's actions, but Leadership needs you to empower your team to reach their potential in the way that best suits them and the agency

- Managers tend to be cautious, while Leaders have to break the rules sometimes and taking calculated risks is part and parcel of the role.

> *Management is efficiency in climbing the ladder of success; leadership determines whether the ladder is leaning against the right wall. (Stephen Covey)*[1]

As a result of these differences, we would argue that the move from Executive to Manager is easier than the shift from Manager to Leader. The shift to Leadership requires you to step outside of your comfort zone, dealing with issues that are not easily 'boxed' and that tend to bleed into one another. That is why it is so important for you to develop your own leadership model which can apply to your agency.

---

[1]Stephen Covey – *The Seven Habits of Highly Effective People.*

4.3. LEADERSHIP RESPONSIBILITIES

The first step in looking at your Leadership model is to understand what you are responsible for as the head of your agency or division.

There seem to be five broad areas of responsibility that agency leaders need to balance every day of the working week. Not surprisingly, these also work as the headline sections of a practical business plan and as the section headings for a 'CEO's To Do List'.

4.4. PEOPLE

The first area of responsibility is People. Do you have the right people, doing the right jobs with the right career progression plan that is linked to the agency business plan? The vast majority of new directors and managing directors are surprised at just how much of their time is spent on people and people-based issues. But when you consider how an agency operates – people selling experience, creativity, contacts and opinions – it should come as no surprise that a considerable amount of your time is taken up with the management and leadership of people.

4.5. CLIENTS

Second are the clients. No, not first. You need to ensure that the right framework is in place to allow your teams to deliver the very best work to meet programme objectives within budget. Along with this, your leadership role requires you to create the right culture within which the teams can operate. This probably means ensuring that your team understands that you will not always put the clients' needs first and that you will take the medium-term view on issues, rather than the 'anything the client wants' approach so many agency heads take.

4.6. PROPOSITION – BEING DIFFERENT

If you've got a motivating culture and are delivering great client work, then you need to start telling your prospective clients about what you can do for them – your proposition and marketing programme. We cover this off in more detail in Chapter 6. Most agencies suffer from being vanilla – they look the same as all the other agencies out there. As part of your agency leadership team, or the head of it, your job includes making sure your agency stands out from the crowd and is on your prospects' agency radar.

4.7. NEW BUSINESS

Love it or hate it, new business – fourth in your list of responsibilities – is part and parcel of every successful agency leader's role. Working out how to convert the leads that your marketing efforts have created is absolutely vital if you have any ambitions to grow your business. If this is not your strength, as a leader, your job is to make sure you build a team that can deliver on new business pitches of all sorts – from stand-up PowerPoint, 'dog and pony shows', to online tenders.

4.8. COMMERCIAL FOCUS

The final major area of a leader's responsibilities, is getting the commercials right. This is not an area that many agency leaders are naturally comfortable with (most of us are promoted because we are good at PR not numbers). But with the right professional input, it can be learnt, and you can become comfortable with making sure the numbers add up.

4.9. LEADERSHIP FRAMEWORK

Once we understand what our areas of responsibility are as leaders, the model of how we will lead becomes clearer. There are hundreds of leadership models available but not all are appropriate for people-centred businesses like agencies.

We have developed our own framework, based on decades spent working in and leading agencies and consulting to a wide range of clients. We should also thank Kouzes and Posner for their book *The Leadership Challenge*[2] which informed our thinking.

The framework is split into two parts:

Part 1 – Action – what you need to deliver to be a good leader

Part 2 – Behaviours – how you need to act to be a good leader

- First tip – consistency wins every time

Let's start with Actions.

4.9.1. Purpose – Vision, Mission and Values

Knowing where the agency is going, and being able to articulate that direction, gives your team something to buy into beyond the usual day-to-day work and team relationships.

Our experience is that the vast majority of your team want to have some form of higher purpose from their work beyond

---

[2]Kouzes and Posner, *The Leadership Challenge*.

Agency

simply earning enough money to pay the bills. This doesn't have to be like a religious experience but something that they can be proud of in terms of your position in the market, the services that you offer and the results you deliver. Most of us want to feel that the work we do makes a difference.

As you know, you are competing in a market for talent that is highly competitive. With retirement ages being pushed back and home ownership becoming increasingly out of reach, the workforce is beginning to look at their careers differently, including what societal benefits their employer delivers. You really need to be looking at your agency as a small community and making sure that it has a purpose.

> *You really need to be looking at your agency as a small community and making sure that it has a purpose.*

Any vision needs to have a significant dose of reality as part of it. Please do not suggest that you want to be the most strategic, integrated agency in the United Kingdom. The best visions are practical but stretching for all the team, supported by a realistic mission and robust and motivating values. The way we look at the three fit well together:

- Vision – where do we want the agency to be in 36 months? That's three summer holidays and three Christmases, which is a time frame that most of us can get our heads round – long enough to drive significant change but not so far away it feels completely out of reach

- Mission – what you need to do to achieve the vision

- Values – how will you and the team behave while delivering the mission? These are best developed with the team rather than created at the top and then communicated downwards.

We would recommend that the vision and mission are kept as company confidential. You need your prospects to understand your proposition, that is the benefits that you deliver for them, but they don't necessarily need to know how you run your company and your ambitions for it.

Your values should underpin your agency culture (see Chapter 3 on Culture) and play a valuable role in your recruitment process and performance reviews. They can also help in the new business process, so should be public.

4.9.2. Innovation

Having set the direction of travel, and behavioural expectations, good leaders find ways of innovating to improve competitiveness of their agency's proposition and to streamline how processes operate internally. If there is one thing we have learned, it is that there is no such thing as the status quo. Businesses only move forwards or backwards. So, without innovation, agencies stagnate and the sector advances around them. This in turn makes it harder to promote an attractive employer brand and attract the necessary talent. Without the right talent, it's hard to win new clients and service them effectively.

> *Businesses only move forwards or backwards. So, without innovation, agencies stagnate and the sector advances around them.*

Introducing new ways of doing things will require considerable support for those members of the team that do not enjoy change. But if they really cannot learn to develop their skills, then it is unlikely that they are well suited to agency life. Overall, we are looking to make effective innovation part and parcel of daily agency life.

At the very minimum, your agency should be researching client demands for new services, developing, testing and commercialising at least one new or updated service a year.

It is well worth remembering that new services need to be driven by market demands not what the agency team is most interested in doing. So, this will require some research and focus to ensure that whatever you develop can be commercialised and sold effectively. As we indicate in Chapter 7 on innovation, there's no point being so smart you are ahead of genuine market demand. As the agency leader, it is your job to provide the roadmap for any

> *There's no point being so smart you are ahead of genuine market demand.*

innovation and to be available to support your team through the process. Regular reassurance, and confirmation of what the desired outcome is, will go a long way to do this.

4.10. BEHAVIOURS

4.10.1. Walk the Talk

Let's not try to avoid the fact that being a leader can be tough. Not only do you need to create the framework that guides the team but you also need to be the example for how you want people to behave, day in day out. When things get tough the need for you to be a role model is even greater.

Put simply, actions speak louder than words. Ralph Waldo Emerson summed it up perfectly when he said: '*What you do speaks so loudly that I cannot hear what you say.*'[3]

---

[3]'Social Aims' by Ralph Waldo Emerson (1875).

This is never truer than in an agency with open plan offices, short reporting lines and informal working practices. When you say to the accounts team you are too busy to do your timesheet or your expenses, or decide to pitch for an account that is far outside of the agency's agreed sales policy, don't be surprised when the rest of the team start doing the same. Don't also be surprised if confidence in the leadership team is dented by you having a public argument with a member of the leadership team. We've not only seen this many times, but have also been told about it many more by disappointed employees.

If your team will copy the worst of your actions, then they'll do the same with your best. If you give thought to what you want your people to do, and how you want them to behave, then you can start to behave in that way. Call it what you want – walking the walk; leading from the front or practicing what you preach – the result is the same. You will be setting the example for the team to follow. That's why in Chapter 3 on Culture, we say it all starts with you.

If the values that the company works by have been developed by reflecting behaviour you know you can sustain, and then live by, there is no more powerful way of building a strong community spirit and the associated reduction in staff churn that this creates.

4.10.2. Motivate

It's a cliché, but agency life can be something of a rollercoaster. The highs are high, and the lows can be very low. You will know from your own career that it takes tenacity and resilience to thrive in an agency. So, as a leader, the need to motivate your team is huge.

The starting point is to understand your direct reports as individuals. While most of us do not want to know every little detail of our team's personal lives, it helps considerably if you have a good idea of what they are looking for out of their career and what they are hoping for out of their personal life.

Beyond that, using tools such as C-Me Colour Profiling[4] and Thomas International's PPA can help you understand how your team prefers to behave at work and give you a guide on how to motivate them accordingly.

Why not take a quick mental inventory of the interactions you had with your direct reports in the last week? What conversations did you have? What were the outcomes of these interactions? Are you happy that you were even-handed, clear on what you wanted and listened to what your team were saying? Did they understand what you wanted, and most importantly, did they commit to delivering it? We use a technique called '*Energy Mapping*' to identify and agree ways to interact more successfully and to play to strengths.

4.10.3. Delegate by Coaching

The ability to delegate is a critical agency management and leadership skill and one that will kill your growth if you don't get the hang of it.

If you are not delegating consistently and effectively, then it is unlikely that you are focusing on the critical issues that will drive agency growth. You also won't be making the best use of all the talent in the agency and not allowing that talent to grow and develop.

The vast majority of agency heads and directors have been promoted as a result of being skilled PR practitioners rather than experienced business managers. Therefore, the temptation to keep dabbling in client work and administration can

---

[4]https://onva.co.uk/c-me/

be irresistible. But there are enough issues for agency heads to be handling without the need to do other people's jobs.

As with many things in agency life, the starting point for good delegation is having a plan. It's vital to define what you are responsible for and how success will be measured. So, if you don't have a clear business plan and Alignment Framework, now is the time to get one sorted.

Once you know what you are responsible for, and so where the bulk of your focus should be going, it becomes clearer what you should not be getting yourself involved in. This is where learning to be an effective delegator makes a huge difference.

Before you decide not to delegate, ask yourself whether there is a team member more qualified to the job? Surprisingly, you probably aren't the best at every aspect of agency management and client work. And, nor will you enjoy doing everything. If you don't let go of certain things, they will drain your energy and motivation – and with it hinder the development of your business.

Even if you think you're still the best at everything, you simply have to let some things go. Would the job give one of the team a chance to raise their profile and add to their knowledge and skills? Are the timescales realistic? Is it likely that the activity will be repeated? If so, it makes sense to plan ahead and see it as permanent delegation. Energy Mapping will identify which actions drain your energy. These are the tasks that you should permanently delegate. If you don't you will get progressively less happy and more tired. You will end up not loving the company you created.

There are some basics you need to get right when sharing the workload. First, explain why it's important the work gets done – the context. The Alignment Framework we discussed in Chapter 2 on Purpose is very helpful here. Second, offer guidance and, importantly, the resources necessary to get the job done. Third, use active listening to ensure people are ready to take on the task. Make yourself available to answer questions and guide people through the task, especially if it is the first time the team member has done the task. Provide specific, clear and constructive feedback on the work that has been delegated to help build the confidence of the individual concerned.

Lastly, don't forget that the 'grunt' work should be shared around. Every agency has stuff nobody wants to do – so make sure you do your share. You'll remind yourself what your team has to deal with day-to-day and they'll respect you more for it. To put this in perspective, we're talking about things like admin you say is essential, such as time sheets!

4.11. PERSONAL LEADERSHIP PLAN

Now we've covered the theory, it's time to create your own Leadership plan.

The starting point is understanding where you are at the moment.

One quick way to do this is to use a spider diagram – see **Figure 1** – to plot how you see your performance against the key Actions and Behaviours. Start by honestly plotting where you think you are currently. Sleep on it and then review it. Better still ask your colleagues to do the same, so you get a full 360 on your leadership performance.

We've used the grades OK, Good and Fantastic. But if you'd prefer numbers or other adjectives that fine. The key is that you have a clear view of how you see your current performance as a leader.

Once you're happy that it's a fair reflection of where you are, you can use it to help complete your own Leadership Development Plan – see **Figure 2**. The idea here is to create a simple activity schedule with clear delivery deadlines that will

Figure 1. Mapping Leadership Performance.

Where am I now?
When do I want to be?

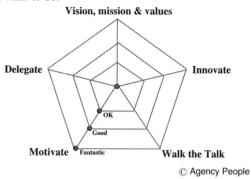

© Agency People

Figure 2. Leadership Development Plan.

Attribute	Score	What am I going to do to get better at this?	Who/what can help me?	By when do I want to do this?
Vision, mission and values				
Innovate				
Walk the Talk				
Motivate				
Delegate				

© Agency People

enable you to improve how you lead your direct reports and your agency.

The actions will be easier to work on – you either have a vision, mission and values – captured in an Alignment

Framework – or you don't. But in our experience, adapting your own behaviour is not so easy and takes focus and a lot of practice. We recommend that you start with one adaptation rather than trying to do everything at the same time. Starting with delegation will have the fastest impact on your working life. It will kill two birds with one stone. It will not only give you more time to focus on what is most important, but also both energise you and motivate team members.

Jim Rohn, an American entrepreneur, summed up the leadership challenge beautifully when he said: 'The challenge of leadership is to be strong, but not rude; be kind, but not weak; be bold, but not bully; be thoughtful, but not lazy; be humble, but not timid; be proud, but not arrogant; have humour, but without folly.'[5] In other words, being a great leader isn't easy. The most important thing to remember is to lead means you need a team that wants to follow.

> *The most important thing to remember is to lead means you need a team that wants to follow. Making your team choose to follow you, is your real challenge.*

The most important thing to remember is to lead means you need a team that wants to follow. Making your team choose to follow you, is your real challenge.

---

[5]'Success Presents Jim Rohn' – https://www.jimrohn.com/7-personality-traits-great-leader/

CHAPTER 5

GREAT CLIENT RELATIONSHIPS ARE BUILT ON RESPECT NOT EMOTION

Issues that may be familiar:

- Client programmes that end up growing in scope with no additional fee

- Demotivated teams running hard to meet changing client demands is damaging growth

- It is hard, if not impossible, to make profit if you don't know what success looks like for the client

At the heart of the vast majority of agencies is a team of creative, hardworking and passionate people. But from a commercial point of view, many of them have a potentially fatal flaw – they like to be liked.

This desire to be liked by clients often results in time being given away for free – the reassuringly named over-servicing. It's also represented by a willingness to live without clear objectives and so results. This produces a definition of success that has a lot more to do with what mood the client was in when they last called.

We may be exaggerating to make a point, but in far too many cases, the relationship between agency and client is more master and servant than partnership. There are many reasons for this – over supply of agencies, lack of commercial skills in agency leaders, low quality of client briefing and low perceived value of PR in the client organisation, to name but a few. But, it is at the coal face, where the client servicing is done, that that the implications of these issues become only too clear.

Too many account teams are put in an impossible position by their leaders. They're expected to balance a continuous stream of client requests, with a fast depleting fee budget, without a clear idea of what they are specifically trying to achieve, how they will know when they have achieved it, and how they will evaluate the outcome.

5.1. COMMERCIAL AND HUMAN

Let's start by looking at the mindset required for successful client service. First, you have to believe that the services you are delivering provide real commercial benefit to your client. You may roll your eyes and ask what on earth are we talking about, but after more than two decades of education of both clients and agencies, there are still a significant minority of programmes that are implemented with robust evaluation.

One of the reasons for this painfully slow and incomplete take up of evaluation by the sector, has to be that the practitioners – both in-house and in agency – do not believe that they are delivering the results expected.

Assuming that you are confident that you expect to deliver commercial value to your clients, it helps to understand that good client handling is a mixture of science, art and emotional intelligence.

If you consider when you last received a great piece of customer service, we bet that your expectations were exceeded by a company or individual that listened carefully to what you wanted, applied their expertise to it and then delivered the service to the required level, on time, within budget and probably added some value on the way.

It sounds simple, but we all know that it is hard to deliver consistently, especially when things go wrong. But consider the component parts of what is required to do this:

- Listening – in the example above, they understood what you wanted and made an accurate record

- Expertise – they applied their expertise to quote accurately and set realistic timeframes. If the service was a bit more complicated – say a house purchase – they would have laid out what they needed from you to be successful. And then they would have kept you up to date with progress

- Added value – having worked out how they were going to deliver what you requested, they drew on their experience to make sure that it was the very best possible service – ideally surpassing your expectations.

This is the ideal combination of commercial and human. The key here being that the commercial part comes first. The service provider's mindset has to be: 'how do I meet (even exceed) my client's expectations while making a profit?' For too many in the agency business, it is pleasing the client that comes first.

We are not suggesting for one minute that the human side of client service is not critical, but it has to be balanced and led by the commercial imperative. After all, if you don't make a sensible profit on the programme, why are you doing it?

5.2. RESPECTED NOT LIKED

This brings us to the next part of getting the right mindset, being respected first and liked second.

The PR agency industry is strange in that we are often bought on emotion. The client liked the team, or they were excited by a big idea that they do not have the bravery or budget to implement, but selected the agency on the back of it anyway. As a result, we are often fired on emotion as well.

This can be tough on the account teams handling the clients because the daily rollercoaster of client emotions, and demands, drives the team's to-do list.

But as expert, commercially led, consultants, it is our job to provide the client with the very best advice on how to achieve their communications goals. This will require you to be a consultant in the truest meaning of the word. Often having to argue for an unpopular course of action or laying out the unpalatable consequences of the client's desired activity.

If you are able to win these arguments, through calm and evidence-led negotiation, you may not be liked but you will be respected. This for us is the start of a great client relationship.

It is much easier to argue your case for commercial reward with a client if you have demonstrated your expertise when it was most valuable, rather than simply agreeing with the wrong decision because you wanted to be popular with the client.

Is this just our opinion? No, it's a fact. Two surveys run by the PRCA highlight this mismatch between what agencies and clients think. In the PRCA's annual benchmarking survey,[1] MDs consistently list the strength of the client relationship in their top three most important attributes for success. In contrast, the less regular, but no less authoritative, client surveys run by the PRCA have client relationships in the bottom three attributes and measurable results consistently at the top.

5.3. SETTING EXPECTATIONS

If you can get your mindset right, then getting the foundations of your client relationships right will be much easier.

The absolute keystone to you client relationship is that both sides have exactly the same idea of what you are trying to achieve, and how it will be measured. Another way of looking at this is asking the question: 'what does success look like?' It's the golden question in our view. If you don't know what will have you, and the client, cracking open the bubbly at the end of the first 12 months of working together, it is unlikely that you will achieve it.

Don't be afraid to ask the question! About 99% of the time, when we ask it, we get a mildly surprised look and the response that the client hadn't really given it much thought. Don't forget that there may be two answers to this question. One that gives the outcome the business wants, and one the outcome your main point of contact wants. You need to know both to succeed.

Figure 1 may seem harsh, but we are confident that many of you will have experienced the impact gap that it depicts — even when outcomes are clearly defined, documented, discussed and physically signed off. So, as you can imagine this

---

[1]PRCA 2018 Benchmark Study.

Figure 1. Identifying the Impact Gap.

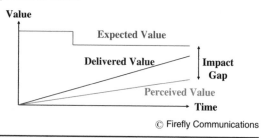

Why expectations matter

© Firefly Communications

gap will grow rapidly if there is no clarity about what is expected from the moment the contract is signed and work starts.

5.4. MEASURABLE OBJECTIVES

We hope by now you will agree that establishing what you are trying to achieve is very important. So, let's run through how you can go about it.

If you want to be able to charge solid fees, and grow a long-term relationship, then connecting your activity to what your client organisation is trying to achieve is a great place to start.

If you are not already asking yourself the following questions, you should be:

1. What is your client's overarching business objective?

2. What are the barriers to, and issues associated with, reaching these objectives?

3. In what areas can communications help address these barriers and issues?

4. What would the communications have to achieve to address these issues?

5. How will we know when we have been successful?

6. What evaluation will this require by us and the client?

7. What should our strategy be for the activity?

8. What are the tactical components of the activity?

9. What is the budget?

10. What resources will I require – both in the agency, within the client and external?

Questions one, five and six are the most important here.

So how do you create an objective that is measurable? There are dozens of ways of doing this, but we will run through a simple example to get you thinking.

We're sure you've all heard about SMART objectives:

- Specific

- Measurable

- Achievable

- Relevant

- Time bound

But in our experience, many campaigns are run without measurable objectives.

Let's apply this model to a credit card business[2] that is looking to increase the number of people who are applying for cards – the business objective.

---

[2] AMEC – *The PR Professional's Definitive Guide to Measurement.*

The communications objective is to attract more prospects to web and social channels to see the benefits that the card offers for themselves.

Based on client data, the prospects we want to reach are AB1 living in London, earning over £35,000 per year and are either renting or a home owner.

The programme is to run over six months and the desired outcome is a 10% increase in applications based on the same period last year.

In summary:

Increase the number of applications by AB1 Londoners earning over £35,000 per year by 10% compared to the same six-month period last year. Do this by communicating the benefits of being a card holder in order to increase the number of visits to the credit card's website and social channels and converting visits to applications.

5.5. KPIs

Once you have your measurable objectives in place you should consider what key performance indicators you are going to use to track progress. They are really designed to identify tactical success.

The KPIs for our credit card example could include the following:

- Increase in positive sentiment around card member benefits on social channels

- Increase in interest and visits amongst target demographic

- Ratios of likes, shares and posts on social media channels

- The conversion rates of different messaging and calls to action

- The number of completed applications by the right demographic.

5.6. CLIENT'S SHOES

You may feel that this chapter has turned into an evaluation lecture, but knowing where you are going, and how you will know you have got there, is central to successful client handling. Just as your business has to have a Purpose, then so does your work for your clients.

Next is to put yourself in the client's shoes. It is all too easy in the hurly burly of agency life to lose sight of the fact that clients are people too, with their own pressures and demands. If you and your teams take a moment to understand what these might be, it will pay dividends in terms of smooth client relations. Few people are without a boss and all of us have to work within the constraints of a budget, often one that is shrinking year on year. Many are expected to deliver more value from the same spend.

Getting under the skin of what makes your client tick is not the same as becoming good friends – you probably have enough of these in your social life. But it is a sensible tactic to help you understand how they will react and why they are behaving as they are.

Helping the client to meet their personal objectives is also a sensible way of building a solid relationship. Understanding what their bonus or next promotion is reliant on can be helpful.

Along with getting a clear picture of what makes your client tick as a person, both at work and home, understanding how the client's internal decision-making process works is a valuable piece of information. This is often driven by their boss and the wider culture of the company.

Once you have a clear grasp of this, you can tailor information, structure reports and timing of requests to give you the best likelihood of success. For example, there really is no point in sending over lengthy monthly reports if they are a company that relies on two-page summaries with clear success metrics. If the budgetary decision-making process is lengthy and involves a number of decision-makers that you do not have contact with, you need to allow for this while planning the next programme or campaign.

5.7. MATCHING THE TEAM TO THE CLIENT'S BEHAVIOUR

Client teams are often made up of those consultants that have capacity rather than those that are best suited to the client in terms of approach and behaviour. While this is a pragmatic approach, it misses out on the benefits of matching behaviours.

We have mentioned in Chapter 4 on Leadership the benefit of understanding what your direct reports' chosen workplace behaviours are, and the same is true for your clients.

There are a number of tools available to help you do this – the ones we prefer are in the footnote below[3] – but with a bit of thought you can make an educated guess yourself.

A few questions to consider:

- Is the client punctual?

- Are they detail orientated or prefer grand ideas?

---

[3] C-Me Colour profiling (https://onva.co.uk/c-me/).

- Do they ask for things in advance or at the last minute?

- How do they like information presented?

- Do they enjoy small talk or get straight to business?

- Do they share information about their home and personal life?

- Are they good at feeding back within timescales?

- Do they share information about their colleagues and bosses?

- Do they enjoy being wined and dined?

- Do they ask or tell people what to do?

- Do they want you to follow tight processes or respond to their latest idea?

When you pull his information together, it provides a useful insight into how they like to behave at work. If you have a detail-oriented, task-focused introvert, pairing them with a gregarious, big picture account director is not the recipe for success.

While we realise that it is not always possible to find the ideal match, if you keep your eyes and ears open from the pitch process onwards, you can plan to get the best possible fit over the lifetime of the client.

5.8. NO SURPRISES – USING SCARF WITH CLIENTS TOO

For most of us, a surprise birthday party is a nice thing. The same cannot be said for the agency client relationship. With a focus on being liked and keeping the client happy, there can often be delays in sharing bad news with clients — account team changes, missed targets, budgetary over-runs, etc.

The delay in sharing negative information is rarely beneficial to the client relationship. So, coming clean quickly and completely is always the best policy. If the account is being operated transparently on both sides of the relationship, then issues should be flagged early and dealt with before they become a crisis.

This does require the respected first and liked second mindset to be in play but that really is the basis of long-term commercial relationships.

We've mentioned the neuroscience framework SCARF more than once. It works for clients too. The 'no surprises' point connects with the need for Certainty — or the need to know what will happen next. That's why contact reports that spell out what will be done are so important. It's also why frequent contact — to avoid nasty surprises — makes for a good client relationship.

5.9. TWO-WAY STREET

Information flow is the life blood of any good client relationship. If we are to be able to deliver objectives on time and on budget, then we are reliant on the client playing their part.

This sounds simple, but it's so important that we want to address it as a specific subject in this chapter. Whatever model you use, it is critical that the client is completely aware of what they need to deliver for you and your team to be successful. Obviously, clients experienced at working with agencies should understand this, but we are always surprised at how agencies are expected to work miracles while working in an information vacuum.

Sadly, not providing you with the information that you require to do the job is often forgotten when the programme's success is being reviewed. So, make sure if your teams are facing this issue, it is addressed early on in the relationship. Using the SCARF model to explain why you need the information can add to the perception that the client is dealing with experts.

5.10. TOOLS

There is a myriad of tools available to smooth out workflows and speed up client service. We do not intend to try and provide an exhaustive list in this book. But, we do suggest you visit PR Stack (https://prstack.co), which provides a comprehensive overview of tools available – both free and paid for.

5.11. ADDED VALUE

If you have clear, measurable objectives, a team that is well matched to the client behaviour and, free-flowing information, you may well be in the position to add some value to the client's business.

Let's get something straight though – added value is not doing more work for free. This seems to be a widely held opinion, and it is one that that will damage your margins and in turn your ability to attract and retain the top talent. We know one agency leader that pushed her team to exceed targets – sometimes by 100%. As a result, she was tired and so was her team. When we pointed out the financial value of the free work being delivered, and what that would mean to her own financial security, two important things started to happen. First, she reduced the over-achievement target to about 10% – still good enough to impress the client but not so much it stressed the agency. Second, she and her senior team started to negotiate bonus payments for going more than 10% over target.

Adding value should come at the point you are delivering on the core programme successfully. If you have insights into the client's business, you can then identify and articulate opportunities for additional projects that will help the client reach their business and communications objectives faster or generate additional revenue.

In turn, this should generate additional, profitable fee for the agency because you are using your expertise to deliver above and beyond the brief. The additional benefit is that, if you truly deliver added value, you will cement your client relationship over the medium- and long-term.

5.12. DEFECTOR OR LOYAL CLIENT – MAP WHERE THEY ARE

The reality is that client relationships will go through their ups and downs despite the agency's best efforts. So, it makes sense to put in place a structured review process that not only takes the 'temperature of the water' but also provides an opportunity for the agency to ensure that the client is fully aware of the range of services included in its proposition.

The vast majority of client relationships fit into one of four categories:

(1) **Defection** – agency's margin and revenue is falling.
   • There are major issues and the account is likely to be out to pitch

(2) **Transaction** – agency's margin falling
   • Agency does what it is asked

- No great chemistry

- In reactive mode

- No wow factor

(3) **Partnership** – agency's margin is rising
    - Team is proactive with the client, providing ideas

    - Client is responsive

    - Client listens to agency and actions its advice

(4) **Loyalty** – agency's margin and revenue rising
    - Agency providing professional and personal counsel

    - Client awarding extra work

    - Client recommends agency

    - Invoices paid without question

The quickest way to collect the information necessary to ascertain where your client relationships sit on this continuum is to ask yourself five questions about the relationship (**Figure 2**):

(1) Are we really delivering on the client objectives?

(2) How do they feel about the account team and the agency?

(3) How do they behave towards the account team?

(4) What style is the communication between the agency and the client?

(5) Is the client relationship a profitable one?

Having got the answer to these questions, the next step is to plot your clients on a simple graph – see **Figure 3**. You may find clusters of clients in each relationship type. Great agencies plan to move every client into a state of loyalty.

Figure 2. Assessing the Quality of Client Relationships.

Assessing client relationships

	Defection	Transaction	Partnership	Loyalty
We do	Let them down	The basics, on time	More than they ask for; in a way that they like	Drive their business results and careers
They feel	Embarrassed	It's OK	They can rely on us; they like us	We're indispensible
They do	Call your competitors	Not much	Award us more business; help us with procurement	Recommend us to other people
Communication style	Limited; e-mail	Transactional; e-mail	More friendly and personal; texts	Warm and personal; texts and visits
Effect on agency finances	Revenue and margin down	Revenue flat, margin under pressure	Revenue rising	Revenue and margin rising

© Agency People

Figure 3. Identifying the Defection Loyalty Divide.

How are your relationships now?

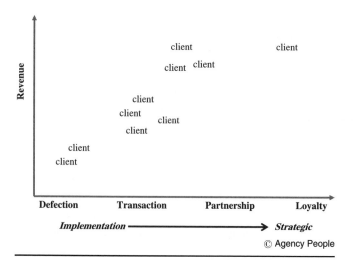

© Agency People

Once you have this information, you need to consider what you would need to do to move the client relationship to the right of the graph and then upwards. In our experience, most account team assessments of their client relationships are normally one category too optimistic.

Initially, you may find that account teams are less than enthusiastic about having their client relationships analysed so transparently. But the benefits should become clear as any grey areas in relationships are identified and plans put in place to address them. Those teams that are struggling with a client in the defection category will be relieved that you are helping to address a relationship that has broken down.

Once the internal analysis is complete, it is time to sit down with the client to discuss how things can be improved or, if you are operating in the Partnership category, what services from your portfolio the client may like to buy.

We suggest that you ask the client to 'score' the relationship using a set of criteria that match what you are offering. These criteria may include the following:

- Support for business objectives

- Quality of strategic thinking

- Application of creativity

- Evaluation of results

- Problem solving

- Effectiveness of reporting

- Effectiveness of communications

This will provide you with the basis for a pragmatic discussion on how to improve or extend the client relationship. The aim is to try and take the emotion out the discussion and provide a framework for an on-going relationship.

It is sensible to give one of your board directors responsibility for the client relationship review process. You should ensure that it is run on your largest fee-paying clients and those that take up the most time or are the most demotivating. You know who they are!

> *No matter how hard you try, there will always be a few clients that are drag on morale, deliver little profit and are frankly just bad for business. Pick one of these each year and fire them. You will be amazed how motivating it is for the team and for you!*

One final thought on client handling. No matter how hard you try, there will always be a few clients that are drag on morale, deliver little profit and are frankly just bad for business.

Pick one of these each year and fire them.

You will be amazed how motivating it is for the team and for you!

CHAPTER 6

COBBLER'S CHILDREN IS COBBLERS – WHY MARKETING MATTERS?

Issues that may be familiar:

- You are short of leads that you want to pitch
- You don't get on pitch shortlists that you are well placed to win
- You win clients that don't motivate you and don't attract other clients of the right type
- Your prospects are not receiving consistent and compelling communications from you
- You have no awards in the cabinet!

For an industry that specialises in communication, we are pretty poor at looking after our own reputations. The normal response we get when we ask why the agency has no focussed and consistently delivered marketing programme is that they are too busy looking after their clients.

The agency is suffering from the 'cobbler's children' effect. We should get one thing straight – 'cobbler's children' is cobblers. An agency that does not market itself is an agency left taking whatever random prospects come through the door or that are passed to them by other agencies that deem them too small, too unprofitable or a conflict with an existing client.

This is no way to run an agency. And, it means you are not in control of where your agency is headed!

It's a clear indication that the agency is being run by the clients rather than the management if the agency team believes it doesn't have the time for marketing. The inevitable result of no marketing activities is that the agency has less choice in what clients it works with, and so in turn finds it harder to recruit quality talent.

> *The concept of 'cobbler's children' is cobblers. An agency that does not market itself is an agency that is not in control of where it's headed!*

So, now that we've cleared up why you need to have a creative, consistent and focussed marketing campaign for your agency, let's agree on what we are talking about.

The dictionary definition of marketing is: '*The act or process or technique of promoting, selling, and distributing a product or service.*'[1]

We will gloss over the fact that it does not include a specific reference to public relations and accept that this works well for an agency. It is all about promoting and selling your services. The best agency marketing campaigns deliver dual benefits – differentiated positioning and the right kind of leads.

---

[1]Merriam-Webster's dictionary.

6.1. VANILLA AGENCIES

There are thousands of Ltd companies in the United Kingdom that purport to be public relations consultancies, and the same is true for the vast majority of developed economies around the world. To be blunt, we have a considerable over-supply. This has ensured that fees have remained low and that there is a shortage of talent – but that is another discussion.

If you take time to identify which of these agencies actually have a clearly differentiated proposition, that is consistently promoted, and provides a platform on which the agency can demonstrate its expertise and experience, we think you'll be looking for a long time.

We can think of a handful of agencies that have taken the time to develop a clear communications strategy and tactical platform and then consistently promote it with creativity and vigour over an extended period of time.

6.1.1. Trust

Let's start with the biggest agency in the world – Edelman. Its annual Edelman Trust Barometer was started in 2001 and is still running today. By 2018 they had surveyed 33,000 respondents across 28 countries. It measures the public's opinion of government, business and media, both traditional and social. It is produced by Edelman Intelligence.

From our perspective, Edelman is the only world top 10 agency that has clear blue water between it and its competitors in terms of promotion and communication. It will probably come as no surprise that the Trust Barometer is directly linked to the agency's proposition:

> *Our proven strategy is to engage audiences over time to earn their lasting trust – the strongest*

insurance against competitive disruption, the
antidote to consumer indifference and the best path
to continued growth.[2]

It doesn't take a communications genius to understand the benefits that this annual communications platform provides Edelman in terms of speaking opportunities, client briefings and workshops, media coverage, social media and talent attraction.

When you look under the surface, it's one of the oldest PR tactics in the world – a survey. A survey well done and well-funded, but a survey none the less. So, if you have been reading this thinking to yourself 'well that's all OK for Edelman they're huge', think again.

No matter how big you are, you have the tools available to build a differentiated positioning and communicate it.

6.1.2. Talkability

This brings us to the second agency we'd like to use as an example of marketing well done – Frank. Frank is a London-based consumer agency now with offices in Glasgow, Manchester and Sydney. The founders of Frank decided to build their proposition around a word they trademarked – Talkability and coined this definition: '*The buzz that takes over and does your best marketing for you.*'[3]

This proposition has been creatively and aggressively promoted for more than 15 years, resulting in an enviable client list, solid year-on-year growth and a plethora of awards.

---

[2]www.edelman.com
[3]www.welcometofrank.com

Whatever the size of your agency and resources that are available to you, it is possible to create differentiation through the development of a compelling proposition.

6.2. A PROPOSITION THAT HELPS YOU WIN THE RIGHT KIND OF CLIENTS MORE EASILY

We can't tell you in this book what your proposition should be, but we can give you some tips on how to develop it:

- *Experience* – start with looking at your experience and track record
  - Where have you been most successful?
  - What do you enjoy doing the most? Don't underestimate the power of a motivated team – and a motivated you!
- *Clients* – what are clients buying at the moment?
  - This is critical if you are to create a proposition that you can convert to cash
- *Prospects* – who is going to buy your proposition?
- *Commercial* – what are the most commercially successful services in the market?
  - The newest and shiniest often don't deliver profitable fees unless, of course, they deliver a genuine breakthrough advantage to clients
- *Delivery* – what are you in a position to deliver with your current team?
  - If you want to deviate more than a few degrees from your current offering how will you resource it – in-house training, recruitment or outsourcing?

- *Context* – what are the current sector trends that you feel have longevity and that you can exploit for commercial success?
  - ○ Getting in too early can mean it is hard to sell and getting in too late can mean that the margins are being depressed by oversupply
- *Differentiated* – who else is selling a similar proposition?
  - ○ Does this really matter? You could argue that both Edelman and Frank are selling the same PR services as their competitors but they have packaged and promoted them in a more compelling way that connected to an outcome that will be valued by prospects
- *Team* – make sure that you get people from all levels of the agency to work on the proposition development
  - ○ You need to make sure that you are garnering input from a team with a range of experience and interests to make sure it is balanced
- *Refinement* – share the draft proposition across the agency and collect structured feedback so that you can refine it
- *Articulation* – makes sure that you have a proposition that you can articulate simply and quickly. Our two examples are Trust and Talkability – it doesn't get pithier than that!

6.3. SENSE CHECK THAT WHAT YOU DEVELOP WILL BRING YOU THE RIGHT CLIENTS

Once you've developed the proposition to the point that you can swiftly articulate it and have the evidence to make it compelling, we recommend that you test it with some friendly current and former clients. This should give you an idea of any issues that an objective interested party may bring up.

You can also make sure that you can answer all of these questions confidently:

1. What am I selling?

2. Who am I selling it to?

3. Why should they buy it?

4. What benefits does it bring?

5. How much does it cost?

6. What objections am I likely to face?
    o Do I have credible answers documented?

One final thought on your proposition, it needs to be robust enough, clear enough and simple enough to turn off as many prospects as it attracts. Not everyone is a prospect and if your proposition isn't clear enough, you'll end up wasting a lot of time with prospects who are not a good fit for what you offer.

6.4. CAMPAIGN DEVELOPMENT – HOPE DOESN'T PAY THE BILLS

It's a cliché, but hope isn't a management tool. Marketing campaigns for agencies do not just happen – you need to take action.

The first step is to draft the brief, as you would with any prospective client. Without wanting to teach grandmothers to suck eggs, you will need to include the following:

- Objectives:
  o Reputational

- o Financial

- o How will you measure the objectives?

- Target audience(s):
  - o Don't forget current clients!

  - o Don't forget current and future employees

- Supporting examples and data

- Proposition summary

- Messages

- Any planned activity

- Timescales

- Budget

- Definition of success.

Once you have a brief you are happy with, we recommend that you appoint an 'account team' from your agency to develop recommendations for a campaign. Ideally, you should treat this like a real pitch, with the appropriate timescales and resources available. If you have the manpower, why not get two teams to 'pitch' and take the best campaign ideas from both.

Just don't fall into the trap, so many clients do, by getting carried away with a great creative that isn't bang on strategy and won't resonate powerfully with your tightly focussed target audience.

6.5. THOUGHT LEADERSHIP – A PLATFORM FOR YOU TO OWN

As a consultative business, it would seem odd if the core of your campaign is not some form of thought-leadership activity.

Edelman has worked hard for more than a decade and half to own Trust in the eyes of professional communicators internationally. While the challenge that you set yourselves may not be quite so expansive, it is important for your agency's success that you are able to identify a theme or platform that you can own.

We often find that agencies are not as creative with their own communications as they for their clients. This is a mistake. Thought Leadership demands that you are interesting and engaging. Don't be one of those agencies that post '10 things we can learn from ....' on LinkedIn. You need to look around the issues that your prospective clients are facing and find ways of bringing them to life.

Having done this, you need to get your thoughts and insights in front of them. This is no easy task, especially with the oversupply of information and agencies.

If you have the reach and the resources of an international agency, such as Golin, you can take David Hasselhoff to Cannes Lions, as they did in 2014, to highlight the importance of relevance in social media. The #HofforNot game reached more than 62 million people before the event and a further 12 million during the 45-minute seminar it was discussed in.

While we have not seen any evidence on the impact the campaign had on Golin's new business efforts, we bet that it made for very interesting credentials meetings and was used to demonstrate the firm's creativity to current clients.

Clearly, very few agencies have the funds for this kind of activity, but, with a little thought and clarity of objective, any agency worth its salt should be able to get themselves on to the radar of its prospective clients.

To be blunt, if you can't do this for yourselves, how on earth are you going to persuade your prospects that you can do the same for them?

6.6. CULTURE – MARKETING FROM THE INSIDE OUT

The best agency marketing campaigns become part of the internal culture and the day-to-day lives of the account teams. No matter whether you have an in-house marketing manager or rely on the account teams to deliver your proposition to prospects, if it is not understood by everyone in the office then it is unlikely to succeed.

You want to be getting suggestions for target prospects from all over your agency and ideas for creative ways of reaching them. We also suggest including marketing activities in six-monthly Personal Development Plans and linking them to the marketing objectives in the firm's business plan.

Having said this, some consultants are definitely farmers rather than hunters. You need these guys to keep the money coming in on the big accounts, so cut them some slack if they do not get on the lead generation bandwagon.

But when the majority of the agency backs the proposition and plays their part in promoting it, you know that you are on the way to developing a culture that will support new business success and help to grow profits. This won't happen overnight, but it is worth being tenacious as the benefits are considerable.

6.7. IMPLEMENTATION NEEDS AN EFFECTIVE PROCESS

You will have your own methodology for running client accounts. We assume that you will apply this to your own marketing activity, but it is always worth revisiting a few of the golden rules of successful campaign management:

- Objectives need to be measurable
  - Set KPIs to track progress of tactical programmes
- Bite-sized programmes – 'eat the elephant one slice at a time'
  - weekly, monthly and quarterly actions
  - team actions combine to create an agency plan
- Celebrate and learn from successes
- Accept and learn from mistakes
  - Written outputs
  - No-blame culture.

6.8. A DATABASE THAT DELIVERS THE RIGHT RESULTS

Most of us have had to get better at handling databases in recent years as the channels that we manage on behalf of clients demand it. While in the United Kingdom, GDPR has made things a bit more complicated, the database is still your friend if you are promoting your agency.

Now that prospects need to opt in to receive communications from your firm, the quality of the resulting database should be high.

Your database should cover the following:

- Prospects
- Clients
- Past clients
- Former employees
- Partner companies

- Friends of the agency – people who will recommend you to others.

Keeping this database updated and meeting privacy regulations will take some resource, but it is money well spent as it should contain your warmest leads and will be the most direct route to your broader prospect community.

6.9. WINNING AWARDS IS NOT ABOUT VANITY BUT CREATING A CLIENT MAGNET

Whatever your views on the plethora of awards schemes that are run every year in the agency sector, they should play a role in your marketing activity. They are great money spinners for the organisers and can be for you as well.

All our experience points to the fact that prospective clients do take awards into account when drawing up shortlists and even when making the final decision on appointment, if all things are equal.

Success in entering awards, like most things in agency life, requires planning, expertise and not a little evidence. You'll need to identify the awards that are best suited to the client programmes you feel are the strongest in terms of creativity and objectively measured results.

Almost all awards now require you to link clear measurement of success to the original campaign objective(s). If that is in place, then the judges will take a look at the creative. But, having judged a lot of awards, in the UK and internationally, we know that many judges will ignore an entry if the evaluation does not match the objective.

There is definitely an art to writing a winning entry – you can even go on training courses to learn it. But have a thought for the judges wading through lots of awards, often more than 30 for a category. Make it an engaging read with a punchy summary that tells the whole story. Only provide supporting material that is relevant. It's a case of quality over quantity every time. You'll need to make time and apply resources to do a winning job. Not only will it support your marketing efforts but it can also help with your recruitment. Who doesn't want to work at an award-winning agency?

6.10. ACTIVATE PARTNERS TO EXTEND YOUR REACH AND TO CREATE WARM INTRODUCTIONS

Relationships are the life blood of successful agencies. This is no different for your marketing activities. If you stop and consider the wide range of relationships that you and your team have, you'll probably find that they are more extensive than you initially thought and that there is a high level of connection between them.

Finding a way to making use of these relationships to promote your agency can really have a big impact on the number of conversations that you can have with prospects. Once you have your foot in the door you'll be well placed to close a sale – but the toughest part is getting the door open.

You'll want to find different ways to activate these relationships. Let's take the other agencies you work with on client campaigns. At the simplest level, this can be a straight forward revenue share for passing on leads that are then converted. About 5%–10% of the first year's fees is not unusual.

If you want to grow the relationship, further joint marketing activities can pay dividends as you are often able to offer a broader, more integrated service which can be more attractive to prospects. Plus, we've always found working with another consultancy team can spark creativity which is otherwise hard to tap into with a team familiar with each other.

Don't forget the contacts of your account teams. They may not know the MD of a prospect but a contact with a marketing manager can pay dividends when accounts come up for review, or you are looking for a way in to a prospect to pitch a creative strategy that you have developed for the sector. We'd recommend that you try and get a plan together for utilising these contacts so that they are contacted with relevant information on a regular basis.

It is all too easy to start an activity and then for it to drop away as the team realise that marketing is often a medium- to long-term activity, without the much wanted short-term wins to keep motivation high. So, make sure you recognise small successes along the way to keep the team energised.

6.11. JUST SAY NO TO PROSPECTS THAT AREN'T AN IDEAL FIT

The prospects that you turn down can be as important to the success of your business as the ones you win. Many years ago, there was an advertising campaign for a tinned salmon brand called John West. It went something like: *It's the salmon that John West rejects that makes John West salmon the best.* This is a principle that we recommend you follow when you are pitching for clients.

One agency owner once asked us if we could help him improve his win rate. He pitched for every opportunity that came his way and won about one in four. We said we could double his win rate with one piece of advice — pitch for half as many! Behind this advice is the fact that his agency's proposition wasn't clear enough to discourage prospects who weren't a good fit, and therefore, he had no chance of winning. There was another reason too. He hadn't identified what his ideal client looked like.

It is always tempting to say yes to the prospect who is promising riches and creative freedom. But you need to ask yourselves some simple questions before committing to pitch:

- Do they fit our sales policy?
  - If not, why are you pitching them?
- What is the probability of success?
  - Is the brief clear with a transparent definition of success?
  - Do we have a budget?
  - Is the prospect's contact professional in their dealings with you?
  - Do we have access to the decision maker?
  - Do we have a track record in the sector?
  - Do we have the right team available to pitch?
  - Is the pitch timetable realistic?
  - Do we know how many agencies are pitching?
  - Is the team engaged with the prospect's proposition and the sector it operates in?
  - Have we been added to the list through recommendation of just a Google search?

If you are getting more negatives than positives, then you are probably not going to be successful. But if you do win the account, you may well find yourself in a working relationship with a client that is demanding more from you than the fee justifies and who is also demotivating for your team.

One of the tell-tale signs of a client that is not going to help your business, is one that suggests you do the first campaign (or year) at a reduced fee with the promise of more money further down the track. In all of our time in agencies,

> *In all of our time in agencies, we have never seen this extra money appear. It really is a case that a loss leader is just a loss in the agency business.*

we have never seen this extra money appear. It really is a case that a loss leader is just a loss in the agency business.

By sticking closely to your sales policy, which should be central to targeting your marketing activity, you will increase your chances of winning pitches. And you will not have to explain to your teams why you are pitching a prospect that is unprofessional before the contract has even been signed.

If the honeymoon is no fun imagine what the marriage will be like!

6.12. RESOURCING – UNTIL YOU IDENTIFY THE COST OF INACTION, YOU WON'T JUSTIFY THE COST OF ACTION

We started this chapter highlighting the fact that making excuses for not having a marketing programme for your agency is a recipe for disaster. We've found that often the reason for this is lack of internal resource. So, it makes sense to consider how you can use an external consultant to promote you to prospects, while you get on with the job of leading the talent, servicing clients, pitching and managing the money.

Using a consultant doesn't have to be expensive, there are plenty of talented freelance PR and marketing consultants who can run with your carefully constructed campaign. You'll get the best results if you handle the relationship in the same way as your best clients deal with you: providing information in a timely manner, being clear on what is working and what isn't, and taking a no-blame approach to evaluating the success of the programme.

In terms of funding, you probably need to consider what the alternatives are to not marketing your agency. They are not attractive. They will help you to identify the cost of lost opportunities. And this will give you the financial justification for a consistent and creative programme. It might also encourage you to stop giving time away free to clients.

6.13. INNOVATION KEEPS YOUR MARKETING AHEAD OF THE COMPETITION

We would like to finish this chapter by banging the innovation drum again. Once you have a robust proposition that you and your team are motivated to sell, and a great marketing campaign to promote it, don't forget that this will need to be refreshed regularly. You should aim to develop, commercialise and launch one new service per year, or you are going to stagnate as an agency. The truth is that agencies have to keep moving forward to survive, and innovation in services is an important part of this.

Marketing your consultancy should be a joy not a chore and if you don't enjoy doing it you are probably in the wrong job.

CHAPTER 7

MAKING YOUR INNOVATION CHOICES PAY-OFF

Issues that may be familiar:

- Your efforts at innovation more often than not fail to deliver significant revenue

- You focus your innovation efforts on client services and ignore internal operations

- Your team aren't enthusiastic about delivering the new services you create

We are often asked how much effort should be put into innovating. It's a very good question. To succeed in such an over-crowded market, it's important to be different. It's more important for that difference to be compelling enough that clients will want to buy it. But how much do you need to innovate to be different?

The PR sector attracts creative people who are always looking to do something new. One agency owner we know – Alberto – is an innovation junkie. He's always looking to be first to market with new ideas. When he has a new idea, or spots something other innovators are trying, he becomes convinced his agency should add this new idea to their service mix. However, his enthusiasm and his conviction aren't always matched by his team. For them, it just feels like another idea they don't fully understand and don't believe clients will want. Over time, this has developed a resistance to new ideas – a kind of 'innovation fatigue' – that thoroughly demotivates Alberto.

To change this attitude in his team, and to re-energise Alberto, we recommended an 'innovation lite' approach that Alberto can connect to the Purpose for his agency and for himself. This focuses on two things in particular:

(1) **The Purpose** – What's the purpose of the innovation, i.e. how will it help the company achieve its objective more easily and with more certainty?

(2) **The Timing** – When is the best time to deploy the innovation?

In the rest of this chapter, we answer the two questions above and the three below:

(1) Should the focus be on innovating services or on innovating internal processes, or both?

(2) Who should create the ideas behind the innovations?

(3) How do you get your team to buy-in to the innovations and use them?

7.1. WHEN IS THE RIGHT TIME TO INNOVATE?

This is an interesting question because there is an answer that is right for the market and an answer that is right for your business. Sometimes – but not always – they are the same answer. Working out when they are different is vital to you achieving the goals you set yourself.

Let's first look at when it's right from a market perspective – with some help from Geoffrey Moore.[1]

Although written for the high-tech sector, the fundamentals of Geoffrey Moore's *Crossing the Chasm* are a good guide for when you want your new services to be available.

If you come up with something completely new, then you have two major problems. Firstly, nobody but you understands what you have created or why they need it. Secondly, even if you can explain the benefits to people, only the 'Innovator' group in **Figure 1** will be likely to buy it. That's just 2.5% of the potential market. This means that you will need to spend a lot of time and effort finding the right people to sell to. It also means you will probably need to sell face-to-face to explain this new concept properly. Even if your sales efforts pay-off with some wins, this success won't translate into other people approaching you to buy the service too because it will be too early for it to be on their needs list.

So, if you're right at the 'bleeding edge', your idea won't be attractive to enough people for it to pay-off. You'll need to put a lot more effort and investment into market education. The result is you could be very smart but also very poor.

So, our advice is to let other people be the trailblazers. Then, ride the wave of a new market, just as the chasm has been crossed (the early majority phase). This way you'll be associated with all the excitement and potential of the growth phase without all the graft and risk of creating the market.

---

[1]Geoffrey Moore's book *Crossing the Chasm* was first published in 1991. It focuses on marketing and selling high-tech products (https://en. wikipedia.org/wiki/Crossing_the_Chasm).

Figure 1. An Adaptation of Geoffrey Moore's Market Lifecycle.

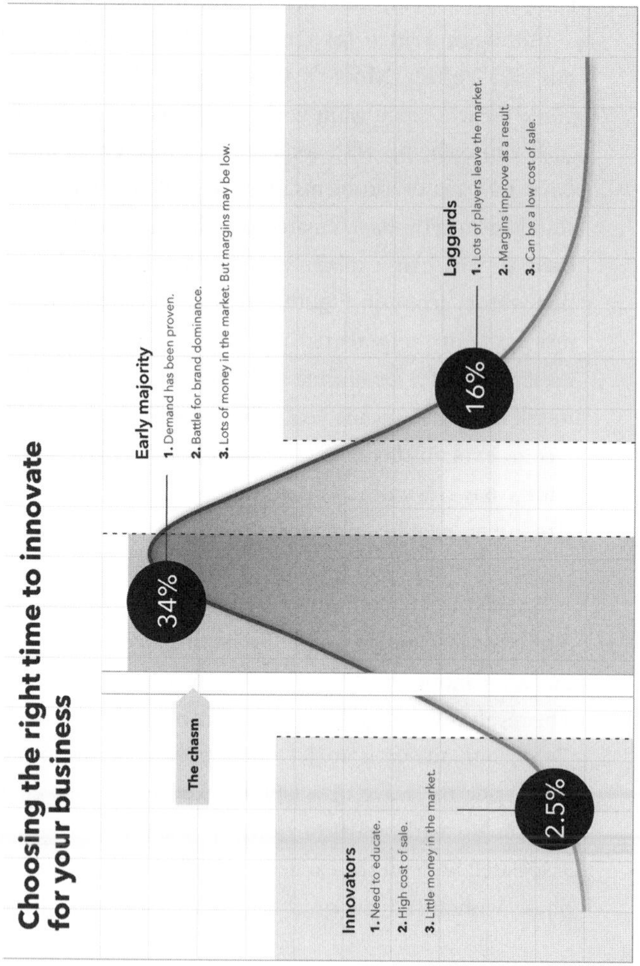

Choosing the right time to innovate for your business

Innovators
1. Need to educate.
2. High cost of sale.
3. Little money in the market.

The chasm

2.5%

Early majority
1. Demand has been proven.
2. Battle for brand dominance.
3. Lots of money in the market. But margins may be low.

34%

Laggards
1. Lots of players leave the market.
2. Margins improve as a result.
3. Can be a low cost of sale.

16%

Then all you need to do is show how and why you would be a better choice than the other players in the market.

This approach also means that your people are less likely to feel that the new services are something they can't deliver. They'll see people just like them delivering them too.

7.2. IS NEW ALWAYS BEST?

In recent years, quite rightly, there has been a lot of focus on moving to digital communications. There has been a parallel debate about the merits of sticking with media relations. Many people believe media relations is dead[2] or at least in terminal decline. So, there is a need to review your service mix and decide where you should innovate.

But before you change everything, it's worth looking at Geoffrey Moore's lifecycle diagram again. The 'Laggard' segment continues to meet a significant market need. The PRCA Census in 2018[3] valued the UK sector at £13.8bn. This makes the Laggard segment worth £2.07bn! It's a segment that usually has many fewer active vendors because most have decided to jump to a new market. So, as many agencies move to the digital world, there could be a very lucrative market with less competition in the media relations world.

You could choose to service this need. Whether you choose to do so or not will depend on your personal and business purpose and how close you are to your exit. We discuss these issues below.

---

[2]https://www.prweek.com/article/1452838/breaking-news-media-relations-dead
[3]https://www.prweek.com/article/1463401/uk-pr-sector-grows-seven-percent-two-years-says-pr-communications-census

7.3. NOW LET'S LOOK AT WHEN IT'S RIGHT FOR YOUR BUSINESS

If you are thinking of innovating, the first question we recommend you ask is: 'Will this increase my chances of achieving my personal and business purpose?' The answer may depend on how close you are to achieving your 'exit'.

A lot will depend on:

- Whether the innovation is revolutionary or incremental

- How much it will cost in money and effort to make the innovation work

- How long it will take for the innovation to pay-off

- What difference it will make to make your business '*good enough to sell*?'

- How near you are to your exit.

Innovation is a choice you make. And it's a choice that has a lot of implications to whether you realise what you want from your business.

7.4. THE IMPORTANCE OF INNOVATING TO ACHIEVE YOUR PURPOSE

If we focus on an innovation's impact on being good enough to sell (Chapter 10), there are a number of possible outcomes. The right idea could be as follows:

- Increase your 'sex appeal' and make you stand out from your competitors, so you become more attractive to acquirers

- Improve your income and profit and provide a clear future income stream

- Increase client loyalty to your brand – because the idea is owned by the company and not one of your team

- Increase the premium you can command from acquirers.

But, it could also:

- Be too early to get the right reaction from clients

- Be a drain on profit

- Be a distraction that negatively impacts income generation

- Undermine the confidence of your team

- Take longer than you want to pay-off.

So, when you are considering investing in an innovation, think carefully about the impact it will have on the business. Use your Alignment Framework to identify where it may add value or why it might not deliver the value you need to achieve your objective.

7.5. THE IMPORTANCE OF GETTING THE TIMING RIGHT

People say that entrepreneurs will risk everything because they have nothing to lose. But if you are nearing your exit, you probably have quite a lot to lose if you make the wrong choices. So, your attitude to innovation will probably take on a different risk profile than if your exit is a long way off.

This is why having clarity about your personal and business purpose is so helpful. And, why knowing yourself – and what this means about the choices you are likely to make – is so important.

> *Remember, you build a great agency one choice at a time. The secret to success is to make sure that the choices you make improve your chances of achieving your personal and business purpose.*

If you are an innovation junkie like Alberto, you will have a natural preference to keep innovating. But if you are nearing your exit, the wrong kind of innovation could derail your plans. So, when we helped Alberto, we kept reminding him about his personal purpose. It didn't stop him innovating but it made him focus on small-step innovations rather than revolutionary ideas.

These smaller innovations collectively had a significant positive impact – a bit like the law of marginal gains[4] that has been attributed to being behind the transformation of the Great Britain Olympic cycling team. The interesting thing about the cycling example is that, for it to work, it needed a culture of innovation/improvement that everyone in the team bought into.

Does that mean that incremental innovation only works as you near your exit? No, it can work at any time and is clearly something that will come from showing that you value every idea that your team creates.

If we focus on the proximity to your desired exit, then you may well exercise different choices about innovation.

- Something with upfront investment and a longer term payback may not be the right choice for you

---

[4]This article in the *Harvard Business Review* describes how small-step innovations were transformational for the GB Olympic cycling team (https://hbr.org/2015/10/how-1-performance-improvements-led-to-olympic-gold).

- But, something that drives revenue and profit would be worth implementing.

Remember, you build a great agency one choice at a time. The secret to success is to make sure that the choices you make improve your chances of achieving your personal and business purpose.

7.6. THE IMPORTANCE OF KEEPING YOURSELF ENERGISED

As we've indicated above, the right kind of innovation can have a very positive impact on business and financial performance. But it can also have a positive impact on you. If you are like Alberto, innovating will be important to keeping yourself energised. If you feel starved of implementing new ideas, you are unlikely to get what you need from your business to keep you happy and motivated.

So, just like when you develop your purpose, we recommend that you look at innovation from the perspective of what's good for you and for the business. That's one of the reasons why one of our innovations is 'Energy Mapping'. It enables you and your team to understand the importance of energising each other.

7.7. SHOULD YOU FOCUS ON INNOVATING SERVICES OR ON INNOVATING INTERNAL PROCESSES, OR BOTH?

Service innovation is more complicated than process innovation for many of the reasons discussed at the beginning of this chapter. There needs to be clear demand for the innovation to pay-off, and it needs to be relatively easy for you to demonstrate your difference. Many of the things that need to work in your favour you can't control.

Internal process innovation you can control. So, it may make more sense to focus attention here.

The funny thing is that, in our experience, very few owners do.

For example, there is usually a lot of focus on sales, but some leaders don't challenge how they sell so they can improve it. For example, we ran a business planning workshop with the management team of one PR agency. We were looking at revenue growth. We asked three questions you may like to ask yourself:

- How many active pitches do you have at any one time? Answer: Usually at least six to 10.

- What is your win rate? Answer: We win about one in four pitches.

- When was the last time you declined to pitch? Answer: We've never declined to pitch (in 26 years!).

The answers show a number of important things:

- The agency must have a good reputation because it's not short of opportunities to pitch

- They are obviously pitching for work they are unlikely to win, or the win rate would be higher

- They are expending a huge amount of energy on new business sales that is wasted — and could be better expended elsewhere

- They haven't a clear idea of what type of client they want to work for or where they have the strongest competitive advantage.

Let's look at those answers again.

- We usually have at least six to 10 concurrent pitches.
  - This requires a huge amount of energy and can become very tiring if there isn't the occasional break from selling

- We win about one in four pitches.
  - Put another way, we lose three out of four pitches. Losing is very debilitating. It drains energy and confidence. It also makes people wonder if what they do every day is worth the effort. As we show later, this can have a very negative impact on mental and physical well-being

- We've never declined to pitch in 26 years!
  - If we draw a military analogy this feels a bit like the charge of the Light Brigade,[5] i.e. we know it makes no sense to go after this opportunity but let's do it anyway. There really is no benefit in being a gallant loser. It's much better to put yourself in the best position to win before you pitch.

There really is no benefit in being a gallant loser. It's much better to put yourself in the best position to win before you pitch.

These answers show that there are compelling reasons to improve/innovate the sales process. Very simple innovations can and have made a positive difference to this business. For example, when confronted with the folly of continuing

---

[5]The charge of the Light Brigade has been positioned as a glorious defeat when it fact it was an example of avoidable slaughter (https://en.wikipedia.org/wiki/Charge_of_the_Light_Brigade).

to pursue the same old approach, the management team agreed to:

- Identify where they are strongest – and stronger than the competition – and focus effort here
- Identify where they can prove the value that they deliver to clients and capture and publish that proof
- Decline to pitch if the opportunity isn't in an area of strength and where they have current proof of that strength
- Update their website to reflect this new focus so they only attract prospects of the right type.

Just taking these steps transformed their win rate and the morale and mental well-being of the team. Now they win three out of four pitches and they expend less effort in doing so. Another positive benefit of this small-step innovation is that the team didn't stop with these important changes. They decided to look at who pitches, how they pitch and what they charge for the work when they win. Each small improvement has made a difference. Unsurprisingly, their financial performance is much improved.

7.8. WHY NOT INNOVATE TO REDUCE OVER-SERVICING? IT WILL BE GOOD FOR YOUR BUSINESS AND YOUR PEOPLE

We've used a sales example because, as our introduction says, it's an area that owners focus on a lot. We could have focused on innovating on how you serve your clients to reduce over-servicing. However, much like the example above, this is an area that most agency owners choose to ignore. Or they tell themselves that by getting the team filling out time sheets is going to address the over-service problem.

In our view, making that choice is a big mistake. It has a very damaging impact on the performance of your people. They soon begin to learn that the hard work they are doing doesn't contribute what it should. It makes them feel like the work has little purpose.

Neuroscientists have proven that having a sense of purpose really matters. Quite simply, it makes us neurologically and physiologically better.[6] So, by choosing not to fix your over-servicing issues, you are actually causing mental and physiological harm to your people.

There are many small-step innovations you could develop to reduce over-servicing and increase the sense of purpose. My own efforts focused on developing a methodology called ValueFlow™ that focused client effort where it would deliver a guaranteed return. We're sure there are smarter ways of doing what we did but, it was good enough to win the firm the accolade of the *CBI's Innovative Company of the Year*. Perhaps more importantly, this innovation gave us a sales advantage at a time when clients needed to be given extra reasons why it was safe to invest in communications.

7.9. DON'T UNDERESTIMATE THE INERTIA THAT CAN COME WITH YOUR PEOPLE

I've seen many agency owners think that the logic behind their idea – and the way that they explained it – will be

---

[6]Reducing over-servicing can improve the mental and physical well-being of your team (https://magazine.vunela.com/why-purpose-works-the-neuroscience-of-meaning-e285cc3bc795).

enough for people to start using it. It isn't that simple. The reality is that you will be subject to reactions caused by their natural behavioural preferences.

Even if your people think your idea is a good one, it doesn't mean that they believe that they can deliver it. Some people — let's call then 'Helpers or Supporters' — will want to support your new approach but they will lack the confidence to do so unless you invest time in helping them prove to themselves that they can do it. If you don't help to get them over this confidence hurdle, they simply won't engage, and you will be left frustrated. Worse still you may see them as unhelpful and wrong for your agency, when they are in fact excellent team members.

> *History is littered with brilliant ideas that didn't pay-off. There will be lots of reasons why — many of which are outside your control. But the one thing you can control is how you involve your people to ensure that they support your idea and help to make it the success that it deserves to be.*

Another group — let's call them Co-ordinators and Observers — will want much more detail about the new idea. How it works, why it's better than other approaches, what to say when people ask questions, etc. Without this extra detail about the process of deploying the innovation, they will lack confidence that the idea will perform as promised.

Then you've got the group — let's call them Reformers and Directors — who will challenge whether it's the best idea or at least think that it's an idea that could be made better. If you don't involve them in the creation or improvement phase, they are unlikely to buy-in.

The final group – let's call them Motivators and Inspirers – will love the idea that you want to do new things. But, like the group above, if you don't make them feel involved in its creation, or the best way to market and sell it, they simply won't buy-in.

History is littered with brilliant ideas that didn't pay-off. There will be lots of reasons why – many of which are outside your control. But, the one thing you can control is how you involve your people to ensure that they support your idea and help to make it the success that it deserves to be.

7.10. UNLOCKING THE INNOVATIVE THINKING OF YOUR PEOPLE

My Father used to say that nobody has the monopoly on good ideas. And he was right. It's very likely that everyone that works for you has at least one good idea that could deliver value to your business. But many won't volunteer these ideas unless you make it very easy to do so.

So, how do you do create a culture of innovation, where people want to contribute to continuous improvement, like the GB cycling example above? Below are five steps we recommend you take to make your business benefit from new ideas.

(1) Show that you value every idea

We know some of you will be shouting at the page that this is bonkers. Some ideas just aren't very good. That's true of course. But, what's more important than the idea itself is that one of your team felt able to share it. For some people, this alone is a huge step, because they fear it may open themselves up to criticism or ridicule. So, if you kill their idea before it has a chance to develop, at a brainstorm for example, you will most likely kill any desire they have to share another.

By showing appreciation for every idea, you will provide the environment needed to enable good ideas to germinate and grow into great ideas.

(2) Make it easy for people to share ideas when they have them

People have ideas at the funniest times and the strangest places. So, it makes sense to make it easy for them to capture and share them with you. There are plenty of apps out there that are designed to capture and share ideas. But, you don't need anything fancy or expensive to benefit from your team's innovative thinking. Engagement Multiplier, the tool we mentioned in Chapter 3 on Culture, has a Suggestion Box feature that will give you all that you need. This includes enabling you to send a personal comment on the idea and what you plan to do next.

You can access a free trial of Engagement Multiplier by following this link[7] (https://www. engagementmultiplier.com/en-gb/partner/onva/).

(3) Provide a focus for ideas

While some people love coming up with new ideas, others need a focus for their creative thinking, or a trigger to share something they've thought about for some time. The fact is, some people don't think you will be interested in their ideas unless you are very specific about what sort of ideas you are looking for. So, if you

---

[7]A free trial of Engagement Multiplier can be accessed here: https://www. engagementmultiplier.com/en-gb/partner/onva/

want ideas on how to save costs, say so. Or if you want ideas on how to attract graduates, say that too.

You may be surprised by the difference the ideas you receive will make. The first time we asked for ideas for a client – as part of an employee engagement initiative – we received ideas from employees that saved £2.5 million in operating costs in the first six months alone!

(4) Show appreciation and recognition in equal measure

We've seen clients and agencies connect reward and recognition to innovation schemes. These are good things to do as they meet many of the needs of the SCARF framework mentioned in Chapter 3 on Culture, such as Status, Relatedness and Fairness.

However, some personality types would rather avoid the limelight that comes with public recognition. Instead, they would prefer a sincere personal thank you that shows that their efforts have been appreciated at the highest level. It's therefore very important to understand each team member's natural preferences, so that your efforts to thank them trigger a friend or reward reaction.

(5) Show what a difference the ideas have made to achieving your business Purpose

Sometimes, people don't share their ideas because they underestimate the impact their idea will have. It's therefore important to show the tangible difference each idea you implement has made to achieve your business Purpose. By connecting your ideas to achieving the outcomes in your Alignment Framework – see Chapter 1 on Purpose – not only will you remind people to stay focused on the Destination for the company but you will also accentuate the importance of the contribution the team member has made by contributing their idea.

So, the moral of this chapter is to focus your innovation effort where it will make the most difference to your ability to achieve your personal and business Purpose. And, to be conscious of how close you are to your exit, so your innovation choices are consistent with the needs of that exit.

CHAPTER 8

NEW BUSINESS – THE LIFE BLOOD OF ALL AGENCIES

Issues that may be familiar:

- Demotivating sales targets – because you never hit them

- Feast or famine approach to new business – all or nothing

- Being asked to pitch for clients that are too small or not in your area of expertise

- Not all of your team are engaged with your new business drive

- Some of your people saying they just aren't sales people

Many a consultant's career – quite rightly – has been built on the ability to develop and present a great pitch and win new clients. New business is the life blood of any agency.

But the pitch is just the visible end of what is an integrated process that includes a number of disciplines, ranging from strategic thinking and data management, through content creation, and sales, to recruitment.

In this chapter, we address the component parts of the new business process. We discuss how to address the culture change that is required to make sure that 'new business is everyone's business' and that the talents of the entire team are applied to winning those all-important new clients.

Before we start on the detail, we should make it clear that we are really talking about sales. Like describing giving our time away for free as over-servicing, agencies call sales 'new business' because it is a more acceptable phrase. But let's not duck the reality – it's sales!

Lots of agency folk will tell you that they don't like to do sales. But it's something that we all do every day when pitching a story to a journalist, presenting ideas and programmes to clients, and internally, as we persuade colleagues to support our ideas.

It takes planning and resources to have an 'always on' new business process. It takes real focus to make sure that this effort isn't wasted.

8.1. TARGETS YOU CAN HIT

The beginning of any new business process must be setting achievable but stretching targets. If they are not achievable, they won't be motivating.

Many of us have experienced the heart-sinking process where the new business targets are delivered from the top, with no regard to the reality on the ground. You and your team are left to figure out how on earth to deliver numbers that are often simply out of reach. The negative impact on morale and motivation from this approach can have far-reaching effects and is very definitely best avoided.

The starting point for your new business financial targets should be the identification of your 'Exit' income. This is the fee income you will start the new financial year with, or the income you exited the last year with. This income should be split between retainers and projects, so you understand which income is recurring and which income isn't.

Set your growth income based on these figures, rather than the gross fee income for the last financial year. Gross figures make no allowance for any changes, such as changes in the economic environment, team changes, the make-up and motivation of the leadership team, along with changes to the mix of retainers and projects.

Having done this — analyse the number of leads that came into the agency in the last 12 months. If you aren't tracking leads, make sure you start now. Track all the leads you pro-actively generate and those that you react to. Then work out the number of leads that became credentials meetings, those that developed into an opportunity to pitch and then calculate the percentage of pitches that you win.

If you have time, take a look at the split of wins that come from traditional 'dog and pony show' pitches, those won by online tenders, those won with procurement involved, and those won when the prospect did not give you a budget to pitch against. You will quickly find out where your sweet spot is.

Identify when in the financial year the wins arrive. Add to this data the average client spend, and you can create a rough calculation of the number and type of leads you will need to generate to hit your new business targets. This will also show you what those wins will deliver in terms of fee.

While we appreciate that this approach is a bit rough and ready, it increases the likelihood of creating targets that motivate rather more than just adding 10% to last year's billings does.

Also, don't forget to work out what you will need to do in terms of recruitment if you grow fee to the desired levels. In a very competitive talent market, you want to be planning your recruitment rather than having to do it in a rush in response to a new client win. You can find more information on this in Chapter 9 on Commercials.

8.2. SALES POLICY – WHERE ARE YOU GOING TO LOOK FOR REVENUE?

Having worked out what your financial targets are, you need to decide where you will go hunting.

Let's get one thing clear – not everyone is a prospect. Difficult as many agency heads find turning down unsuitable leads, as Alberto discovered, a little bit of focus, and the ability to hold your nerve, will pay dividends in the medium term and long term.

Your sales policy needs to focus on prospective companies that you will be most credible pitching to. Your pitch credibility comes from a combination of team experience, agency case studies, your services, location, price and relationships.

Of course, you want to be ambitious in entering new sectors. But this is often best achieved through the introduction of a new service and associated thought-leadership. We cover this in more detail in Chapter 6 on Marketing.

When it comes to building your database of prospects, you ideally want to know their:

- Sector issues and trends

- Business objectives

- Past use of agencies and associated spend

- Location

- Culture

- Job titles

> *It is extremely beneficial to make sure that everyone in the agency understands what your ideal prospect looks like. That means everyone from the apprentice and graduate trainee to the accounts team. You'd be surprised how many leads are uncovered when the agency understands what a good one looks like.*

Add to this list prospects for any new services that you have in the works, and you have the makings of a workable sales policy.

At this point, it is extremely beneficial to make sure that everyone in the agency understands what your ideal prospect looks like. That means everyone from the apprentice and graduate trainee to the accounts team. You'd be surprised how many leads are uncovered when the agency understands what a good one looks like.

8.3. LEAD BONUSES NEED CAREFUL PLANNING AND TRACKING

You may wish to consider putting in place a bonus for those team members that bring in a lead – this will mean you have to track them all accurately!

The bonus could be a one-off payment after the first month's fee has been paid or a percentage, say 5%, of the first year's fee.

For the record, we don't believe that team members should be bonused for pitching prospects. This sits firmly within the day job. As ever, with bonuses you have to consider the behaviour you want to encourage, rather than what you like as a manager or what other agencies are doing.

Use the SCARF framework to guide you when you are putting a lead bonus scheme together. It's particularly important that you make sure the scheme is seen as fair to the whole team. If you don't make sure it is seen as fair, something you hope will have a positive impact on the agency, could end up being divisive.

8.4. VANILLA AGENCIES FIND THAT SELLING IS HARDER

Having worked out how much fee you want to bill, and who you want to sell to, it's important to make sure that you stand out from the crowd with a clear and compelling proposition. If it doesn't turn off as many prospects as it attracts, then it isn't clear and compelling enough. Remember, trying to be all things to all people means you'll blend into the crowd.

You don't want to be running a 'vanilla' agency. Nice, but bland is hard to get excited about. We aren't saying that every agency has to be double chocolate chip, but you can be raspberry ripple – solid with a twist.

We cover this off in detail in Chapter 6. Despite the number of competitors out there, it's very possible, with a little thought, to differentiate. Your difference can come from a number of areas, including activities such as the development, commercialisation and launching of new services, custom methodologies and strategic partnerships that aid the delivery of client objectives.

8.5. CREATING A PITCH-READY AGENCY

There have been many great books written on the art of the pitch – *Life's a Pitch* (Bantam Press) and *Presentation Magic*

(Marshall Cavendish) to name just two – so we are not going to cover the topic in too much detail.

Having said that, do we want to share the component parts of developing a pitch-ready agency.

As with so many issues in agency management, much of this is cultural rather than operational, although getting the right processes in place provides a platform to shift the agency culture in the direction you want to.

From our perspective, the seven-component parts of a pitch-ready agency are as follows:

1. *Right people mix* – you really need to recruit to sell. This means a good mix of introverts and extroverts, big picture and detail-orientated and as diverse as possible.

   There are lots of tools on the market that help you understand how your team prefer to behave while at work, but two we have used with great success are C-me[1] Colour profiling and Thomas Personal Profile Analysis.

2. *Sales strategy* – have a clear one and make sure everyone understands it.

3. *Lead generation* – an ongoing and consistent programme of activity. We are often asked about developing a lead generation programme. One of the simplest ways is to draft a brief as a prospect would, and then treat your agency as a client. You will be amazed at what ideas are developed when you take a step back and look at your organisation dispassionately.

4. *Team selection* – again, you can use tools to help identify how the prospects prefer to behave and try and match your team accordingly. For example, you'd want to avoid

---

[1] https://onva.co.uk/c-me/

pitching with a team of extroverts if the key decision-maker is an introvert.

5. *Pitch content development* – a simple and documented process should be in place to ensure that when a lead arrives it is assessed objectively and swiftly and, if you are pitching, a clear timetable established. You want to make sure that maximum time is available to identify the all-important insights and develop the creative platform to exploit them.

While the macho all-nighter may seem fun to the more junior staff, it is not the best way to develop a compelling strategy or award winning programme. We'd recommend you take the following approach:

- Carve out time in the diary to research, develop and rehearse the pitch

- Make sure the brief is understood by all the team – in detail!

- Get going on the budget and pricing early. We often see the financial element left to the end and then rushed

- Accept you will have some dead ends creatively – it's part of the process! But get out of the office to be creative. Unusual ideas hardly ever surface in the usual places

- Focus on learning everything you can about the prospect, its issues and operating environment

- Don't compromise on the strategy – make sure it is based on real insight and lends itself to deliverable and affordable creative platforms

- Rehearse, rehearse and rehearse

8.6. NO-BUDGET TENDERS AND OTHER ABERRATIONS

While many older practitioners will tell you it was better in their day, the honest truth is that new business pitches have always been something of a crapshoot. Poor briefs, flawed client decision-making processes and stupid timescales, have always been part of winning new clients.

Having said all of that, it would seem that the last decade has seen the introduction of a number of practices that makes the job of winning a client that much harder.

Pure-play online tenders with no opportunity to speak to the prospect or garner initial information or insights are common. Prospects requesting strategies and programmes without providing access to the details of their business or organisation are not going to get the best result for them or the agency. But this is the world in which we operate. It is up to you, as the agency head, to decide how you want to play the game.

For example, your sales policy should reflect whether you will pitch without a budget being provided, or whether you will pitch for prospects when a procurement team is involved. Whatever you decide to do, make sure it is a conscious decision and plan accordingly. So, if you are going to negotiate with a detail-orientated introvert from procurement, do not send in an extrovert, big picture agency director – unless you've given them special training to handle this situation. You need to learn how to deal with different types of prospects and work out which you are best at winning.

One last point on pitching without a budget. While we know this is now a common practice, it is simply stupid! How on earth do you make informed decisions on the type of programme, resources to assign, or what impact you are trying to deliver, without knowing how much money you have to spend? We both know of agencies that simply refuse to pitch without a budget, and while you do have to hold your nerve, you tend to get more professional clients with this approach and increase your win rate.

8.7. PIPELINE MANAGEMENT FOR BOTH NEW AND CURRENT CLIENTS

While planning your lead generation activity, it is always useful to have a process to take prospects through − pipeline management if you will. We have tried a number over the years but none seem to fit the agency model precisely, although we found that the Pace Partners model has many of the components required.

Our process has six segments, which you move prospects through:

1. *Prospecting* − a database of all your prospects that you have yet to contact

2. *Contacting* − prospects that you have had contact with but are not yet in dialogue. For example, they have signed up for blog posts or a newsletter

3. *Needs analysis* − by the time a prospect gets to part three they are qualified − they fit the sales policy − and you are in dialogue with them to identify how you might help them

4. *Pitching* − a list of current pitches and a process that gives you sufficient time to do a brilliant job

5. *Creating loyalty* − as we detail in Chapter 5, successful agencies are adept at building loyalty in key clients

6. *Saying no*− what to do with those clients that are over serviced or are bad for morale. We would suggest swift

action to fire them or address the problems. A bit of judicial client pruning will be very popular with the client teams and do wonders for morale.

8.8. GROWING EXISTING CLIENTS

It is often said that the quickest and cheapest way to grow your fee is to get more money from the clients you already have. While this is true, your starting point when planning to grow your current client fees should be to accept that not all clients can be grown. Some don't have the budget. Your relationship with others will not be strong enough to give you the 'right' to grow the fee.

We'd suggest that rather than set a blanket growth fee target across all your client portfolio, cross-selling or up-selling is only attempted once you fully understand the quality of your relationships.

Agency and client relationships normally fit somewhere on this range:

- *Defection* – major issues, unhappy client and account out to pitch

- *Transaction* – agency does what it is asked, not much chemistry, no wow factor

- *Partnership* – agency is proactive with the client, chemistry is good and the client listens to advice from the agency team

- *Loyalty* – agency provides professional and personal counsel, client awards projects, recommends the agency to prospects and pays on time.

8.9. CLIENT LOYALTY

In our experience, the best way to gauge the strength of a relationship is through a face-to-face meeting. Ideally, this should be with someone that is not involved in the day-to-day work on the account. If the fee is sufficiently large, an outside consultant can be used.

There are many online client loyalty surveys, but these often deliver very low levels of response and do not allow you the opportunity to gauge body language or the nuances of the conversation with the client. We aren't saying don't run a client feedback survey. But we are saying this should supplement the face-to-face approach rather than replace it.

If you approach these conversations in a structured way, you can compare the findings across your client base. This can be done with a questionnaire or spider diagram, which allows you to plot client satisfaction with key components of your service, ranging from delivery and proactivity, through value for money to strategic thinking.

It's best to avoid discussions around whether you are creative enough unless you have specific examples to discuss. No client in our 60 plus years of combined experience has ever felt their agency had an excess of creativity!

Once you have identified areas that the client feels require improvement, the next step is to draft the account development plan. This should definitely be done with the account team and then discussed with the account director and client. The key point here is to ensure that the remedial actions that are identified are actioned swiftly and that the client reaction is then gauged.

By following this process, you can not only address client concerns and so, in turn, strengthen your working relationship, but also create opportunities to present your wider portfolio of services in follow-up meetings. It is our experience that clients that feel they have had their concerns taken seriously, and actions have been taken by the agency to address them, are open to expanding the services they buy from the agency. This is because of the psychology of surprise. By listening to them, and acting on their feedback, you will most likely positively surprise them. Positive surprises create a willingness to try something new and to recommend.

8.10. SUMMARY

It is a cliché, but agencies really are like sharks — they do not survive for long without moving forward. Winning new clients is at the core of creating this momentum, so the need for a comprehensive programme that starts with recruiting the right people, and finishes with knock-out pitches, is a must. You really can't leave something as important as this to luck.

> It is a cliché, but agencies really are like sharks — they do not survive for long without moving forward. Winning new clients is at the core of creating this momentum. You really can't leave something as important as this to luck.

CHAPTER 9

THE MONEY MATTERS – IT'S WHAT AGENCIES ARE REALLY ABOUT

Issues that may be familiar:

- Lack of clear financial information

- Problems with cash flow

- Problems collecting debts

- Over-servicing client programmes

- Problems getting teams to be more commercial

- Lower profit margins than you would like

'*To be honest, I joined a public relations consultancy to write business plans and draft budgets*' said nobody, ever.

But understanding how to plan and manage the finances of your agency is at the heart of good management, not to mention your own financial security.

The vast majority of us were promoted for our expertise in the practice of public relations rather than our ability to manage a business and its financials. So, it comes as no surprise that many become directors, and then agency MDs, CEOs and owners, without any formal training in business or financial management.

This chapter is designed to provide you with insights into the areas of your business' finances that you need to understand and monitor. It also provides guidance on the questions you need to be asking your advisors.

We should say at the start that we are not accountants and that you need to take expert advice before making financial decisions. But that is not to say that we don't have a wealth of experience in what you need to be looking for, and when and how to use this knowledge.

9.1. PICKING THE RIGHT ACCOUNTANT

The starting point for most agencies is appointing an accountant to, at the very least, handle your annual tax return, and if you are big enough and based in the UK, your Companies' House filing.

Like agencies, not all accountants are the same. So, you need to find one that will fit your specific needs and style of working. Most importantly, you want one that understands your Purpose and has the skills needed to help you to achieve it. A bit like your favourite clients, you will get along with the accountant that is right for you on a personal level and who has a similar approach to business.

The first question to ask is whether they have worked with agencies before. If not, you will have an education job to do before you can start to benefit from their expertise. PR agencies are very individual businesses with specific requirements. If your accountant has not worked in the sector before, he or she may have a steep learning curve. We would always prefer our advisers/suppliers to do their learning on someone else's dime.

Second, the way in which they work will make a big difference to the success of the relationship. You need an accountant that is flexible enough to fit with the way in which you want to work but also expert enough to tell you what you need to know. This includes your legal responsibilities, guidance on how to report internally and what ratios to keep a close eye on.

The last significant criterion for selecting and working with an accountant is cost. It is our experience that professional fees vary quite considerably, so make sure you know what fees and associated costs you are committing to. You need to understand whether the fees include bookkeeping, providing management accounts and your annual return. You also need to know what format the reporting will be provided in and how often.

9.2. CAPTURING FINANCIAL INFORMATION WITH AN ACCOUNTING PACKAGE

The ubiquity of cloud-based accountancy packages, Xero, Sage and Quickbooks to name just three, means that it is easy and affordable to collect, track and analyse your financial information. And of course, you will be able to invoice swiftly and in a timely manner direct from the package. You will also be able to track fees and profitability from your desk or on your mobile phone while you are out and about.

Most accountants will have a favourite package, and it is sensible to use one that your accountant is familiar with. But make sure it provides the information that you require in a format that you and your team can understand. You do not want to be transferring data from your accountancy package into excel and re-formatting it so that it is easier to understand.

The good news is that these online packages are mostly provided on a monthly fee basis, so they do not require upfront capital and are not a significant drain on cash flow. Plus, they can be tailored to provide specific reporting formats. This can often be done by your accountant. But if needed, a quick Google search will give you access to package specialists who will help you out on a freelance basis.

9.3. KEEPING ON TOP OF CORE INFORMATION

The good news is that the agency business model is a fairly simple one. So, you do not require a huge amount of complicated information to allow you to make sensible informed decisions on everything from people — recruitment, development and promotion — through to marketing spend and office costs.

> *But it's vital you have your finger on your agency's financial pulse. We've both known too many agency owners who left this to other people — only to find out they've run out of money — or worse still had it stolen from them.*

But it's vital you have your finger on your agency's financial pulse. We've both known too many agency owners who left this to other people — only to find out they've run out of money — or worse still had it stolen from them.

There are six main sets of information that you will need:

(1) **People costs** — This should include all of your people costs, including your permanent and freelance staff salaries and all the associated costs, from gym membership through to pension payments.

People are going to be your biggest single cost — equating to 55%–65% of your annual fee, so it is critical that you have an accurate record of what they are costing the business.

(2) **Overhead costs** – This needs to be everything that is not a people cost. These will equate to 20%–25% of your annual fee, so it is critical to keep a close track on everything from your office rent, IT costs and subscriptions, through pitch costs to client entertainment.

(3) **Fee forecast** – This is the heartbeat of your financial reporting. You need to be able to see fee spend by client by month, both confirmed and being negotiated. This gives you the most realistic fee forecast for the year. This fee can be described as 'Identified and Committed' and 'Identified and Uncommitted'.

(4) **New business** – This covers the fee that you are pitching for and the shortfall (Unidentified and Uncommitted) between your annual target and what fee you have confirmed and are negotiating.

Forecasting your fee and pitch pipeline, this way will give a very clear indication of progress over the year. It will also show whether your initial growth targets were realistic (see Chapter 8 on Sales for details on setting growth targets).

If you have significant changes in your team or a big client loss, it is best to revise your annual targets, rather than blindly ignoring reality. It is much more motivating to hit a revised target than missing the original one due to circumstances beyond your control.

The reality is that agency life is always something of a rollercoaster, and the best planning processes and operational frameworks will not stop the ups and downs. They will help flatten them out a bit and help your respond to them and maybe even see some of them coming, but they will be there nonetheless.

(5) **Profit and loss** – The fifth component of your financial reporting is the actual and forecast, profit and loss. Over

time, it will become clear if you have seasonal changes in your profit or loss. These can often be driven by the sales profile of your clients' businesses. If they have seasonal peaks and troughs in sales, they are likely to spend on their PR accordingly.

> *Of all the figures you need to keep a close eye on, cash is probably the most important. It is a lack of cash that kills agencies!*
>
> *The key to stress-free success is to build an agency that generates cash. This means you won't need to rely on an overdraft to pay your salaries!*

(6) **Cash flow** – The final part of the financial jigsaw for agency heads. Cash flow is something you must keep a very close eye on. This is what you have in the bank at the beginning of the month plus what is forecast to come in and go out during the month. Of all the figures you need to keep a close eye on, cash is probably the most important. It is a lack of cash that kills agencies!

The key to stress-free success is to build an agency that generates cash. This means you won't need to rely on an overdraft to pay your salaries!

9.4. REPORTING FORMATS THAT ARE EASY TO UNDERSTAND

You need to be able to review your financial information swiftly. You also need to be able to explain it to the less numerate members of your board and senior account teams.

With this in mind, we recommend that you produce six separate sheets:

(1) People costs

(2) Overheads

(3) Fee forecast

(4) New business pipeline

(5) Profit and loss

(6) Cash flow

While these should be simple to understand, it often helps to add a one-page dashboard that is designed to appeal to the more visually minded members of your team.

The dashboard can provide a snapshot of the agency's performance from the beginning of the financial year to the current month (year to date), the month you are reviewing and the forecast for the rest of the financial year.

Data that could be shown on the dashboard include the following:

- Fees billed

- Profit or loss

- People costs as % of fees

- Overhead as % of fees

- Fee forecast

- Fee required to meet annual target

- Conversion rates – number of leads received/generated – number of leads that become credentials/briefing meetings – number of pitches won.

Along with the data, the dashboard can also provide a short commentary on the numbers. This often works best when it is split into 'Good News' and 'Bad News' with appropriate icons. While you do not wish to infantilise your senior team, it does no harm to make sure that they do not leave the monthly financial review meeting without a very clear idea of what has gone well and what hasn't.

This allows you to make a short list of actions, with separate owners, for the next month. Remember SCARF and the need for certainty and autonomy. This could be a particular pitch, a reduction in overheads or a review of specific people costs. Our experience is that fixing financial issues within an agency requires commitment and focus. Suggesting that *'We'll sort it next month'* is not the answer.

The key to reporting is to make sure that you are getting the information you require to take decisions about the business. So, if your original format is not working, change it.

It's critical you have the information you need every month. You will sleep much better when you know exactly where you are money wise.

9.5. FORECASTING SO YOU DON'T GET ANY NASTY SURPRISES

One of the areas we get asked about regularly is how best to forecast fees. We have used and seen many different ways of doing it.

But you want to consider the following, when developing your forecast model:

- How you weight the likelihood of winning a client?
  Your past performance of converting leads to clients will help with this. Add to that, identifying a few simple criteria that indicate a greater likelihood of success, such as:

- ■ Do we have access to the decision maker?

- ■ Do we have a budget?

- ■ Do we have experience in this sector?

- ■ Is it a warm referral or the result of a cold call?

- ■ How many agencies are pitching? Etc.

- What stage you are at in the sales process.

- The warmth of the lead – Is it cold, warm or hot?

Having developed your model, it is worth getting into the habit of reviewing the forecast once a month. Any more than this and you start spending too much time re-forecasting and not enough time generating leads and pitching. You are really looking to develop a model that provides you with information that is 80% accurate. You will never get 100%, but you need data that is reliable enough to be the basis for other financial decisions.

It is also worth tracking where the income is coming from in terms of retainers and projects. The average percentage of fees from projects in the UK is currently 40% according to the PRCA's Benchmark Survey. This percentage share of your income is expected to grow. If your agency is facing the same change in the type of your income, then it will have implications for your recruitment strategy and how you manage your fixed overheads. You will need to build in flexibility to your people costs and overheads, or you may find yourself running out of cash.

9.6. CAPACITY – WHAT IS THE TRUE REVENUE CAPACITY OF YOUR TEAM

Another piece of information that makes running your agency considerably easier is knowing a lot about the revenue capacity of your people. This includes knowing:

- How much of each team member's time has been sold to clients

- How much each hour is being sold for

- What time they are spending on client work, new business, people management, etc., each month

9.7. HOURS AVAILABLE TO SELL

The starting point for planning your capacity is working out the number of hours you have available to sell. You can do this by working out the following:

- Number of working days and hours in the year. Work on working days of seven-hour duration

- Number of days of holiday your team has. Don't forget national holidays, any accrued holiday and maternity/ paternity leave

- Allowance for an average number of sick days each year.

Taking the UK as an example, this would give each member of client handling staff 223[1] days a year to sell or 1,561 hours.

But of course, you cannot sell 100% of your team's time. You need to allow for personal development and training, administration, new business, marketing and general social-isation. A rough guide to the percentage of a working week you can sell by job role is:

- Account executive – 80%

- Account manager – 65%

---

[1]This allows for eight public holidays, 25 holiday days and five sick days.

- Account director – 60%

- Director – 55%

9.8. HOURLY RATES

If your local trade association produces an annual bench-marking survey, you can use this as a guide to the hourly rates that you should be charging. But the best way to work them out is to take the cost of your people, your overheads and the number of hours that you have available to sell and calculate what the hourly rates need to be to deliver your desired profit margin. Your target profit margin will depend on what services you provide and sector you work in, but at least 20% should be your aim.

However, as we indicate in the chapter about being 'good enough to sell', the calculation above should only really give you the minimum you should be charging. The more you can prove the value you deliver to clients, the more you can charge. We aren't great fans of cost-plus budgeting. This tends to lead to an attitude that says you need more people to generate more revenue and profit. In fact, as Chapter 7 on Innovation and Chapter 6 on Marketing show, you may just need to have smarter and more differentiated services to be more profitable.

9.9. CAPACITY PLAN

When developing your plan, try and keep it as simple as possible. If you are starting from scratch, an Excel spread sheet can be used to record all the information you need. As with all financial information, this should be reviewed formally once a month.

You will want to track the following information each month, by team member:

- Hours forecast to be spent on individual clients and actual hours spent on clients

- Hours forecast to be spent on marketing and lead generation

- Hours to be spent on new business and pitches

- Holiday that has been booked

- Training/coaching that has been booked

9.10. USE TIME SHEETS TO DRIVE THE RIGHT BEHAVIOUR

There are a wide variety of different systems on the market that will track hours spent and produce reports for you.

But before you install a time sheet system — and 'crack the whip' to get people to complete it — ask yourself how you will use the information it provides. Our advice is to make timesheets all about personal development (so people get better at their core skills) and personal effectiveness (so they get better at delivering important outcomes). This way you can create a culture of self-improvement where each individual reviews their own performance to see if they are improving the way they do things and delivering the right kind of value. If everyone improved by just 10%, the financial impact will be transformational.

By connecting timesheets to both personal and business outcomes, you will need to spend less time on a culture change programme that educates all of the agency on why completing their timesheets every week, ideally every day, is so important. It'll be much more obvious how their actions can help to deliver the financial results required to deliver their much wanted pay rise, promotion or bonus.

But remember, your people will take their lead from you and your senior team. If you don't complete a time sheet, and if you don't talk about the changes that are being made because of the analysis of timesheets, then your team probably won't complete it properly either. In this case, it will just become another wasted exercise. This not only will detract from billable activity, but will also demotivate your people.

9.11. DON'T 'CON YOURSELF' WITH YOUR CLIENT BUDGETING

Once you know how much time you have to sell, you will want to make sure that you are budgeting correctly when you are pitching for new name clients or projects for current clients.

This is not a difficult job but will take a bit of time when you start. You want to avoid combined team day rates. All that will happen is that the client will tend to contact the most senior members of the team and so burn through the day rate, leaving you carrying a loss.

A client budget needs to detail all the planned activities in the programme and assign hours for each team member to them. Do this for the first month and then for a typical month afterwards. The first month should be budgeted for separately as it will invariably require more hours to ensure that the agency team is up to speed with the client business.

Getting the budgeting right means that you will be planning a level of work that fits more closely with the budget the client is spending. If you consistently do a lot more work than the client pays for, then you will rapidly erode your profit margin, demotivate your people and yourself. This

> *If you accept a client with a budget that can't support the work you do, then you're just conning yourself and your people. You can only sell your time once, so you may as well sell it for as much as you can.*

comes back to being firm about the clients you want to win. If you accept a client with a budget that can't support the work you do, then you're just conning yourself and your people. You can only sell your time once, so you may as well sell it for as much as you can.

9.12. OVER-SERVICING IS THE ROAD TO FINANCIAL AND EMOTIONAL RUIN

Over-servicing is the single biggest reason why agencies do not make as much profit as they want or need. The average UK agency gives away 18% of its time for free.[2] That's very nearly one day a week. Fridays really are free! It doesn't take a genius to work out that you will make a lot less profit if you are giving away this much time and our experience is that the amount of time given away is often considerably higher. Let's convert this into money. Imagine you've been growing fast, and you just hit the magical £1 million income figure. It ought to be a time for celebration. But if you've giving 18% of your time away free along the way, you've just walked away from £180,000! That's not something to throw a party for!

There is a straightforward model that you can use to ensure that you give away as little time (and money) as possible. The virtuous circle in the diagram below is not just a pipe dream it can be achieved.

---

[2]2018 PRCA Benchmark Survey.

> *Imagine you've been growing fast, and you just hit the magical £1 million income figure. It ought to be a time for celebration. But if you've giving 18% of your time away free along the way, you've just walked away from £180,000! That's not something to throw a party for!*

Assuming you have a robust client programme budget, the starting point is measurable objectives for all client campaigns. We deal with this in detail in Chapter 5 on Client Handling. But to put it simply, if you can't measure when you have been successful – reached your objectives – it is almost impossible to know how many hours you will need to get there (Figure 1).

9.13. DON'T BECOME A YES PERSON

The delivery of the programme is where the vast majority of the problems arise. As an industry, we have traditionally been very poor at pushing back when clients have requested work that is outside the agreed programme. It is this extra work that results in over-servicing. The answer is to train your team to negotiate, to understand that the work that they do for the clients has a real value and to value each hour that they work for clients.

This is, again, a cultural change from the norm and will require solid and consistent leadership from you and your senior team. It will also need training for the whole team in evaluation, negotiation and budgeting. Those team members who do not engage with the training and show little interest in the commercial side of agency life should not be undervalued as practitioners but are unlikely to be good director material.

Figure 1. Productivity, Profit and Growth.

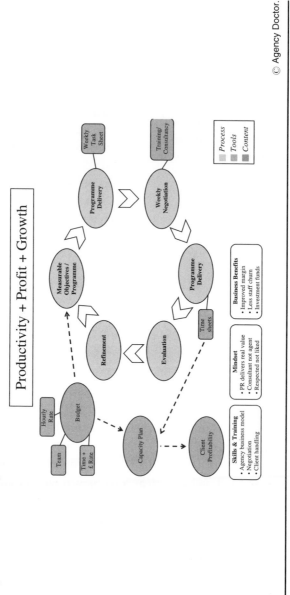

If you can drive this change in attitude and provide the right tools – budgeting, capacity plan, evaluation and time sheets – then you will have the constituent parts of a profitable agency.

9.14. BUFFER

Once you have the agency business model working smoothly – or as smoothly as is possible in a sector often driven by emotion – then you will be generating cash which you can invest in your business, but only after you have taken your well-deserved dividends.

Our starting point would be to make sure that you have funds on deposit that will pay your salary bill for six months. This cash buffer will give you considerable flexibility in making decisions. It will give you the courage to not feel beholden to unprofessional clients. It'll enable you to deal with unproductive and demotivating team members more quickly.

9.15. BY FOCUSING ON THE NUMBERS, YOU CAN BUILD A GREAT AGENCY – AND HAVE FUN DOING IT

We started this chapter by suggesting that nobody joined the PR consultancy sector to write a business plan or develop budgets. But all agencies – whether they like it or not – are businesses. The successful ones don't just win awards for creativity; they make solid and consistent profits. Those profits can be used to reward employees, give a return to shareholders and invest in growth. Agency leaders have a duty to understand their finances and to learn to enjoy handling them. If you don't, you will face a difficult and uncertain future. If you do, you stand a very good chance of building a great agency and having fun doing it.

CHAPTER 10

MAKE SURE THE BUSINESS IS GOOD ENOUGH TO SELL – FROM DAY ONE

10.1. AKA – HOW TO MAKE YOUR BUSINESS ATTRACTIVE TO ACQUIRERS AND YET SO GOOD THAT YOU DON'T NEED TO SELL IT

Issues that may be familiar:

- Your senior staff are earning similar amounts to you for a lot less stress

- You are not making as much profit as you would like

- You aren't attracting the right talent or blue-chip clients

- You are forever struggling for cash

In 'Introduction', we said that you need to make sure that you focus on the numbers and YOU – and not just your people and your clients. We talked about the importance of making conscious rather than unconscious choices.

151

In Chapter 1 about Purpose, we focused on the importance of working out what you want from your business —
both the tangible and the intangible outcomes that will make
you feel you've achieved something special.

In this chapter, we talk about being good enough to sell.
This is not because we think everyone should sell. We don't.
You could give the business away, or just close your doors
one day. That's your choice. And that's what this chapter is
all about — making sure you have that choice. And, that in
exercising it, you feel that you have achieved the goals you
set yourself.

10.2. START BY VALUING YOURSELF AND THE VALUE YOU DELIVER

Michael Gerber,[1] a small business guru, is attributed with
saying: '*The only reason you start a business is to sell it. And
if you don't sell it, all you're doing is buying it with your
own blood, sweat and tears*'.

The trouble is most of us don't think about selling our
business when we are going through all the excitement of
starting it! But we should. It will help us to build a better
business and be more satisfied with what we have created.

If you start with a goal that you're going to sell one day,
some remarkable things begin to happen. You start to think
about ways to make the business more valuable — from
day one.

---

[1]Michael Gerber: https://en.wikipedia.org/wiki/Michael_Gerber_(non-
fiction_writer).

And you start to think about what, and who is valuable — and how much other people will value you.

These thoughts about value — even before you open for business — will be critical to the business you create.

Judith is a case in point. She ran a very big agency for a big group. One day, when her kids were finished at university, Judith decided to start her own company to deliver personal consulting at the highest level for FTSE100 companies. She already had clients who wanted to work with her when she set up her agency. So, she had to decide what she would charge them. She had two choices:

(1) Charge the same fee rate she charged at her big agency

(2) Charge a lower fee rate because her new agency had much lower overheads.

Which option did she choose? Which would you choose?

Judith chose option #2.

If you choose to run your business according to a cost-plus business model (i.e. where you work out your costs and add a profit margin to work out your fees), then option #2 is a perfectly logical decision. But if you choose to charge according to your proven value (i.e. what people are prepared to pay), then option #2 makes no sense. It's a choice that undermines your value.

In Judith's case, clients expected to pay a high fee for her advice. They were used to doing so. So, why not just charge what they are used to paying? If this produces very high-profit levels, then happy days! Suddenly, you have many more choices about what you can do next because you have the funds to do so. And, perhaps more importantly, you have proven to the market, and to yourself, that you are worth the higher rate.

Because Judith was very good, she started to attract new clients. This meant she needed to hire new people and take on new offices. Suddenly, her low fee, cost-plus, model didn't look so logical. Her margins plummeted, and she felt she was working for nothing. She knew her clients should be paying more but, having accepted a low fee, she didn't know how to get it up to the right level.

So, we went to her largest client and re-negotiated the contract. We asked for double the agreed day rate. The client said: '*We were thinking more along the lines of a 10% increase, not 100%*'. We replied: '*In normal circumstances 10% would be more than fair, but you know you've been getting away with the steal of the century for the last two years. All we are doing is finally charging the correct rate.*' Because Judith was genuinely brilliant as a PR consultant (a vital ingredient in this story), the client agreed, and the fee was doubled. At a stroke, the company was back on track.

If Judith had chosen option#1 from the outset, her business would have been stronger, and she would have avoided a lot of angst. And, her business would have been a lot more attractive to an acquirer.

This is one small example of how thinking about value at the outset can help you to focus on doing the right things. If you do – hey presto – you have a business that's worth buying.

10.3. BUILD IN VALUE BY THINKING FROM A BUYER'S PERSPECTIVE

So, what are the right things to do? There are some obvious answers and perhaps some that are less so. The first question to ask yourself is: 'If I was buying this business, what would I want to buy?'

The obvious answers would include the following:

- **Growth**

  You'd want to see both the top line[2] and the bottom line[3] growing. Otherwise, you might be buying a 'dead duck' – or at least a sick one. That's why, in the introduction, we said we talk a lot about growth. You'd want to see growth for many reasons, including:

  - A growing business obviously has something people think is worth buying – that's enough to make you feel more confident about the future

  - It means the business has momentum – something that is hard to inject if it isn't there already

  - It shows that someone or some people are good at selling – another confidence boost for the future

---

[2]Top line: We mean the income that sticks to you and doesn't just flow straight through your business because you are buying in other products or services. Some owners mistakenly focus on turnover, that is, the total of everything they invoice to clients. While this makes the company feel bigger, it is masking the true performance of the business. An acquirer will not value turnover. They will remove this from their calculations. As an example, let's assume a client asks you to buy £250,000 of adverts for them. From a turnover perspective, this makes you look much bigger. But from an income perspective, £250,000 doesn't exist – just what you charge to buy the adverts for the client. So, while some may think this makes them more attractive to an acquirer, the reverse may be true. Because you are buying the adverts, an acquirer may think you have more risk of bad debts, that is, not being paid by your client for the adverts.

[3]Bottom line: This is profit – sometimes called earnings before interest, tax, depreciation and amortisation (EBITDA). It's worth looking at that long list of letters because they all relate to the choices you make – such as purchasing equipment, property or other agencies or how you finance your business.

○ It implies that there are reasonable levels of client loyalty
and retention – again a foundation for a stronger
future.

- **Profit**

You'd want to see a healthy profit. Otherwise, after one
or two bits of bad news, such as a couple of clients going
away, you might be buying a loss-making business. So,
you'd want the profit to be real and not 'propped-up' by
choices made by the owner.

Another agency owner we know – Ian – fell into the
trap of creating the illusion of profit. Ian was desperate to
be profitable. So, he chose to pay himself very little to
produce a profit at the end of the year. This meant that
other people on the team were earning more than him. It
also meant he chose to charge lower fees than he needed
to. For the first couple of years, Ian told himself it was all
fine. He was growing, and he was profitable. But in real
terms, he wasn't, and the false profit showed through in
cash issues. He was running the business on an
overdraft – an expensive and deeply insecure thing to do.
Ultimately, he began to resent the fact that all his hard
work wasn't turning into value for him personally.

So, we asked him to go right back to the Purpose of the
business. We asked him to think about what he wanted
the business to help him achieve. Amongst other things, he
wanted to put his two children through university in the
United States. Now that's £500k of anyone's money. And not
something you can deliver on an account manager's salary!

By helping Ian realise why he set up the business, it
made it much easier for him to make some value-based
decisions. Suddenly, he had a powerful reason to charge
more and to pay himself more.

By the end of the next financial year, Ian was on a
proper MD's salary for a company of its size. The profit

had increased fivefold. The overdraft was eliminated, and the business had grown by winning better-quality clients, paying higher fee rates. For the cynics amongst you, who think that sounds too good to be true, it's true.

Of course, it needed the courage to charge more. It needed hard work to win and keep new clients. Both of these things came from the commitment[4] Ian made to himself – to deliver the future he wanted for his children.

What had been missing was a sense of *purpose*[5] that drove what Ian did. Once he discovered his personal *purpose*, the rest was relatively easy.

- Security

If you were buying, you'd want to see some good contracts in place – with clients and employees. Otherwise, you might be buying past rather than future income. And, you might find you lose the people you need to deliver the return on investment you want.

Chapter 9 on 'Financials' and Chapter 2 on People should give some good guidance on how you create a more secure future income stream.

The PR space has many charismatic owners who are creative and great with clients – but hate the admin work. Successful owners recognise this gap in their leadership skills and 'partner' with someone who fills that gap. Our advice is to have this partnership in place from the outset. It doesn't mean that your admin partner has to be equal

---

[4]See the psychological effect of Commitment and Consistency in the chapter on Purpose.

[5]Purpose: Here, we refer to the personal purpose for the business, that is, the value the business will deliver to the owner. This is different to the business purpose, that is, the value the business delivers to its customers – and inspires its employees to come to work.

with you. It just means they must be on the team and they
must believe in the commercial *purpose* for the business.

- **Sex appeal**

  If you were buying, you'd want to see some cachet
  clients (for the sector you are targeting) and some award-
  winning work. Otherwise, what you're buying might be
  too boring to attract future clients. The latter is probably
  more important. That doesn't mean if you're not working
  for Google you can forget being valued. But it does mean
  that if you don't get recognised for good work, your value
  will be less.

  We know the leader of a very successful agency called
  Diane. She has a relatively low ego and thought industry
  awards were just 'fluff' and vanity. Diane thought that the
  success of her agency was self-evident. After all, she owned
  one of the fastest growing agencies in the UK. So, for
  years, she didn't enter awards – despite the fact that her
  firm delivered results for clients that would have been
  award-winning.

  One day, Diane lost a pitch for a client she really
  wanted to win. She knew someone on the inside at
  the client company, and it turned out the winning
  agency was chosen because they had a string
  of awards. Once she calmed down, Diane
  realised her mistake. While the competitor had
  made their value very explicit, the value
  delivered by Diane's firm

> *So, if you want a high
> valuation, don't hide
> your value. Have a
> dedicated effort to make
> it as explicit as possible.
> This will require time,
> resources and skill. But
> if your work is good it
> will attract new clients,
> the best people and,
> potential acquirers.*

remained implicit. The awards inspired trust in her competitor – they acted as very clear 'trust indicators'.

So, if you want a high valuation, don't hide your value. Have a dedicated effort to make it as explicit as possible. This will require time, resources and skill. But if your work is good it will attract new clients, the best people and potential acquirers.

10.4. BUT BUYERS WANT MORE THAN THE OBVIOUS

However, if you're buying, you'll be much more demanding. You'll look beyond the obvious answers to see if a premium is worth paying. And if you're selling, you'll want to command a premium!

We've covered some key points in the bullets below. Each one starts with a view from the buyer in italics and then discusses what that means to you.

- **Enough overhead to be a bigger profit opportunity**

   Although you like the look of the profit that is declared, you'd want to see an opportunity to unlock some more. A buyer will look for what we call 'hidden' profits. For example, the buyer will have their own admin team. So, some or all the cost of the one they're buying could go straight to the bottom line!

   Does that mean we are recommending that you build a big admin team? No. It means we're recommending you understand the choices you make about having an admin team – whether it's in house or outsourced. If you chose to run lean because you think that will make you a better profit, then think about the consequences of that choice. Who will do the admin? If it's you, is that the best use of your skills? Is there an 'opportunity cost' associated with you doing that work? Will it energise you or drain your energy? An acquirer won't care. They'll just see the hidden profit opportunity or lack of it.

So, think about the consequences of your 'hidden' profit choices, because they may be undermining your ability to increase your value still further.

- **Client loyalty to the brand, not individuals**

  You'll know that when people sell, they've already decided to leave. But you won't want the clients to leave with them.

  The trouble is that many agency owners focus on making themselves indispensable, rather than focusing on making their agency indispensable. And that doesn't just apply to the owner, it applies to the account owners too. This allows clients to focus on the individual who serves them rather than on the value the company delivers.

  So, if you're a buyer you'd want to see a branded way of doing things that lives on when people leave. We're not saying you need to build a process-driven business. We are recommending that whatever your approach, everyone in the business follows it. And better still, that the approach is clearly unique to your business.

- **Services in growth areas**

  You'll know that growing in a static or declining market will be tough. So, you'll be looking to acquire some skills and services that will bring future growth with them.

  Does that mean you have to constantly innovate? No, constant innovation is tiring and expensive. And, sometimes, new ideas may be too early to make any money – see Chapter 7 on Innovation.

But it does mean that you need to evolve what you have to ensure you are still connected to the new services clients want to buy.

- **No skeletons and poison pills**

    You won't want to pay for someone's poor cash management, tax dodges, IP traps or bad property decisions.

    The great thing about having a clear Purpose from the outset is that it makes it clear when a decision may threaten that Purpose. The examples from Ian and Diane show two examples of how this can happen.

    Another example that abounds in the PR sector is a bad property decision. Without a clear purpose to drive your choices, it's easy to be persuaded that you need a certain kind of office. Most buyers won't be interested in long-term leases on property. Unless, on very rare occasions, it satisfies a need for space. It's more likely they'll see it as a profit drain.

    So, when assessing property, ask yourself what the consequences of each property decision will be. Will the choice make it easier or harder to achieve your purpose? Another owner we know, Andy, decided to take on a 25-year lease for his existing office because the landlord was offering a great deal. The problem for him was his business outgrew that office two years later! And, he couldn't find anyone to take it on. While he managed to secure some sublets, there were many periods when it was empty – causing a

Some people think phrases like 'cash is the lifeblood of any business' is a cliché. It's not. It's probably the most important lesson for anyone starting an agency to take onboard.

cash and profit drain on his business and an energy drain on him.

Our advice is to not create the proverbial skeletons in the closet. No matter how appealing they may sound, ultimately, they will undermine the value of the business and undermine the enjoyment you get from running the business.

- **Plenty of cash**

    You'll know that if there are good cash balances, it's likely the business generates cash. That'll be important to help fund the changes you'll want to make to drive future growth. And, it'll help to pay for the company you are buying!

    We mentioned Ian and how he ran his business on an overdraft until he connected with his Purpose for the business. Some people think the phrase, 'cash is the lifeblood of any business' is a cliché. It's not. It's probably the most important lesson for anyone starting an agency to take on board.

    We've seen agencies that should have been great successes wither and die because the leader didn't focus on the cash. Many agencies' cash management is so dire that they use factoring to stay afloat. Factoring has the benefit of immediate

    > *Many agencies' cash management is so dire that they use factoring to stay afloat. Factoring has the benefit of immediate payment of a big percentage of each invoice you raise, but charges a double-digit interest fee for the privilege. Factoring is like the crack cocaine of the finance sector. Once you're hooked, it's almost impossible to get off.*

payment of a big percentage of each invoice you raise, but charges a double-digit interest fee for the privilege. Factoring is like the crack cocaine of the finance sector. Once you're hooked, it's almost impossible to get off.

We're helping one agency leader called Jon to do that. It's a painful process but we're almost there. He runs an agency with £2 million in fees and £100k in finance costs! In other words, a bank is getting most of the dividend he could be distributing. That's definitely not why he started his business. So, why did he let it happen?

The simple answer is he didn't understand the power of cash, so he didn't make collecting cash on time central to achieving his Purpose. As a result, the bank is the beneficiary of all his hard work. Until that changes, it means Jon has very few choices. By the end of the year – three years into the project – we will have reversed the numbers. About £100k in finance charges will become £100k in cash balances. Jon will have his business back. He's able to do that because he now has a reliable admin 'partner' whose primary focus is on cash management. And, because he has made it the responsibility of his account handlers to assist the cash collection process.

- **Strong succession**

    You'll know that the owner may have built the business, but they won't grow it further. You'll want to see that there is a next generation of people who are already the agents of growth. That's why our Chapter 2 on People focuses so much on involvement and engagement.

    Unless you begin to share the load, with people who are happy to carry it, you will create your own glass ceiling. If you want every decision to go through you, that's fine. This book isn't about being right or wrong. It's about doing the right things to achieve the Purpose you defined for the business.

Our goal is to help you to understand yourself, and the consequences of your choices, well enough to increase the probability that you will make choices that are good for you and your business.

And perhaps the most surprising answer of all would be:

- **Owners who are rewarded at a very high level**

    You'll know that if you can pay someone to run the business less than the owners have been taking out of the business, you will unlock even more value!

    This is counter-intuitive for many agency owners. It certainly was for Ian. He thought paying himself less was a good thing, when, in fact, it was stifling the development of his business.

    This last 'answer' brings us back to the subheading for this chapter: *How to make your business attractive to acquirers and yet so good that you don't need to sell it.*

    If you run the business in such a way that you can afford to reward yourself well, then there will probably be less motivation to sell. You're very likely to earn the same returns as if you sell. With two key differences:

    - You and not the acquirer will be in control of how much you earn

    - You will have developed the next generation of people who can run the business and may have the motivation to buy it from you.

However, if you decide to sell, then your rewards in the past will represent another hidden profit that will justify a further premium for your business.

Now look back up that list of answers. If you saw a business like that, you'd probably want to buy it. And you'd probably expect to pay a premium to get it.

Now look again. Something else will become clear. If you're running a business like that you're probably earning as much as you might if you tried to sell! That will give you a lot of choices about how you eventually decide to realise the value of what you've created.

So, what's the moral of this chapter? Focus on creating value from the outset and capture what that value looks like in a Purpose for the business and for yourself. Use the Purpose to guide your choices and you'll avoid the mistakes made by Jon, Ian, Diane and Andy.

You'll build a great agency, one choice at a time. And you'll have fun doing it!

REFERENCES

CHAPTER 1

[2]https://en.wikipedia.org/wiki/Robert_Cialdini

[3]https://en.wikipedia.org/wiki/OGSM

[4]https://www.gov.uk/write-business-plan

CHAPTER 4

[1]Stephen Covey – *The Seven Habits of Highly Effective People*

[2]Kouzes and Posner, *The Leadership Challenge*

[3]'Social Aims' by Ralph Waldo Emerson (1875)

[4]https://onva.co.uk/c-me/

[5]Success Presents Jim Rohn – https://www.jimrohn.com/7-personality-traits-great-leader/

CHAPTER 5

[1]PRCA 2018 Benchmark Study

[2]AMEC – *The PR Professional's Definitive Guide to Measurement*

[3]C-Me Colour profiling (https://onva.co.uk/c-me/)

CHAPTER 6

[1]Merriam-Webster dictionary

[2]www.edelman.com

[3]www.welcometofrank.com

CHAPTER 7

[2]https://www.prweek.com/article/1452838/breaking-news-media-relations-dead

[3]https://www.prweek.com/article/1463401/uk-pr-sector-grows-seven-per-cent-two-years-says-pr-communications-census

CHAPTER 9

[2]2018 PRCA Benchmark Survey

CHAPTER 10

[1]Michael Gerber — https://en.wikipedia.org/wiki/Michael_
Gerber_(non-fiction_writer)

INDEX